Barbecue Cooking
The Gourmet Way

PATRICE DARD
Barbecue Cooking
The Gourmet Way

◨ METHUEN

Toronto New York London Sydney Auckland

Copyright © 1984 by Les Éditions de l'Homme,
Division de Sogides Ltée.

First English edition 1986.

Published by arrangement with Les Éditions de
l'Homme, Division de Sogides Ltée.
Original title: *le Barbecue*
Translated from the French by Gaynor Fitzpatrick

Canadian Cataloguing in Publication Data

Dard, Patrice.
  Barbecue cooking the gourmet way

Translation of: le Barbecue.
Includes index.
ISBN 0-458-80110-0

1. Barbecue cookery.   I. Title.

TX840.B3D3713   1986   641.5'784 C85-099962-6

Text and cover design: Don Fernley
Cover photo: Jean-François Amann

Printed and bound in Canada

1 2 3 4   86   90 89 88 87

CONTENTS

INTRODUCTION

A LITTLE CULINARY ETYMOLOGY

There are conflicting theories about the origin of the word *barbecue*. Some claim it goes back to the buccaneers, who roasted pieces of meat *de la barbe à la queue* (from head to tail), hence *barbe à queue*, anglicized to *barbecue*. Other experts claim the original word was *barbacoa,* of Iroquois origin and meaning a wooden frame used as a support for roasting meat. They claim the Spanish conquerors borrowed the word and passed it first to the English and then to the French.

A third group associates it with the Spanish word *barbacoa*, meaning a hearth built of flat, heated stones. It originated in Mexico and was adopted by the Spanish invaders. In French the similar word *barbaque* means a poor-quality meat and also comes from *barbacoa*. It was introduced into the French language by the troops sent by Napoleon III to occupy Mexico in 1862. We all know about poor food in the military!

Today, however, much has changed, and regardless of the origin of the word and the method of cooking, barbecues are often gastronomic delights.

THE BASIC UTENSIL — THE GRILL

Grilling food is as old as the discovery of fire. One might even state, without fear of contradiction, that when our paleolithic ancestors began to roast their meals over a flame, the foundations of civilization were laid. Now, a few millennia later, grilling is no longer the only available method of cooking meat; but it is still the surest way to produce the light meat dishes of *nouvelle cuisine*.

But how do we go about grilling our food? And how can we get the most out of our food and our equipment?

There are many types of outdoor cooking equipment. The most inexpensive are portable open grills and hibachi-type grills, and most of the recipes in this cookbook can be used with these. However, if you want to have more control over the cooking heat and a larger cooking surface, covered "kettle-type" barbecues enable you to grill, roast, bake, and partially smoke what you cook. A simple spit and drip pan can be used with any fire, including one in your fireplace. We particularly recommend those barbecues with both a grill and a spit.

These types of barbecues use wood and charcoal as fuel, and you might want to try some new types of wood that are becoming popular in the United States. Mesquite, hickory, and grapevines all impart their own special flavors to grilled foods. Mesquite chips and charcoal, as well as hickory, are best used to grill robust foods like pork, beef, and some seafood. Grapevine cuttings add a sweet, delicate flavor to fish, poultry, lamb, veal, and vegetables.

There are plates and grills made especially for gas barbecues that give excellent results and will last a lifetime if they are properly maintained. Of the electric grills, the infra-red models seem to function best. Solar grills should be considered with caution. Their principle seems to be perfect, but it will be up to your judgment and experience to estimate the cooking times required.

THE PRINCIPLES OF BARBECUING

☐ The equipment, especially the grill, should always be scrupulously clean. It should be scraped with a wire brush after each use, preferably while it is still hot.
☐ It is important that food be lightly coated with olive or peanut oil before it is grilled.

☐ The food to be grilled should be at room temperature, not just taken out of the refrigerator.
☐ We recommend that you season with salt only at the end of the cooking time so as not to draw the juices out of the meat.
☐ Never grill over flames, always over coals—flames burn the meat and give it a bitter taste.
☐ A hot fire has low flames and a red glow. A medium fire has a red glow and no flame; the coals are covered with a gray-white ash. A slow fire has gray-white ash and no red glow under the coals.
☐ The distance from the coals to the grill depends on the meat being cooked. The thinner a piece of meat, the faster it should be cooked, so the closer to the coals it should be. Thicker pieces should be cooked more slowly — farther from the coals.
☐ Beef is cooked closer to the fire than lamb, and lamb closer than pork.
☐ If you like your meat extra-rare, or *bleu*, it must be well warmed before you place it on the grill; otherwise, it will remain cold in the centre, and this is very unpleasant.
☐ If you cook fish, then use the same grill to cook meat, be sure to clean it first. The reverse is less important, but it should be done anyway.
☐ Wooden skewers, especially bamboo, seem to be more suitable for brochettes than metal ones.
☐ Pork fat is often better if it is baked in the

oven a little before being used in brochettes.

☐ Some vegetables, like peppers, mushrooms, and potatoes, should be blanched before being grilled.

☐ Fish, poultry, meat, and game all benefit greatly from being marinated. Consequently, we have suggested a number of marinades suitable for each kind of meat.

☐ Wait until the grill is very hot before placing food on it.

☐ Never pierce a piece of meat with a fork, or it will lose its juices and become dry and hard. Use a spatula or tongs.

☐ It is preferable not to scale fish before grilling. Scales prevent scorching and protect the flesh.

☐ Fish should be carefully wiped and completely dry before being brushed with oil or marinade. Water, oil, and fire do not make a happy *ménage à trois*!

☐ For basting meat or anything else to be grilled, the best tool is a brush, and the best brush imaginable for barbecuing is made by tying together a little bundle of thyme, bay, and rosemary twigs.

☐ Barbecuing fish requires special attention because errors quickly take on catastrophic proportions. Large pieces should be cooked on a hot grill, small ones on a very hot grill.

☐ It is wise to use a hinged double grill to hold fragile pieces of fish so they can be turned without breaking.

☐ Flat fish like sole should be grilled white skin down first.

☐ You can steam fish over the barbecue by covering the coals with damp seaweed, or you can smoke it lightly by cooking it on a bed of water-soaked breadcrumbs that covers the fire, or by smothering the coals with hardwood sawdust (never pine or cedar sawdust).

☐ Cooking in foil (*en papillote*) also offers many advantages. We give a number of recipes using this method, which consists of sealing an ingredient in aluminum foil with various herbs, spices, and condiments and cooking it on the grill or burying it in the coals.

NOTES ON COOKING INSTRUCTIONS

Taste is an individual matter; there is nothing wrong with enjoying your fish a little pink, your duckling markedly rare, or a steak well done, even if this does flout current convention.

For extra-rare (*bleu*), place the meat on a very hot grill, cook for 30 seconds, and rotate it 90°. This quarter-turning allows a crust to form. After 30 seconds turn the meat over and repeat on the second side. The meat will feel soft when pressed with the fingers.

For rare, proceed in the same fashion as for extra-rare, but leave the meat longer on the grill. When a pink juice appears on the upper side of the meat, it is ready to eat. When pressed with the fingers, the meat will offer some resistance but will remain elastic.

For medium rare, turn the meat as before but move the grill farther away from the coals. Cook until drops of juice appear on the upper side of the meat. The meat will still be a little elastic to the touch but will be noticeably firmer than the rare piece.

For well done, proceed exactly as for medium, but keep the meat on the grill until an almost chestnut-colored juice forms on the upper side. The meat will be noticeably firm to the touch.

When grilling white meat (chicken, rabbit, veal, pork, etc.), quarter-turn as for red meat and cook until a clear juice appears when the thickest part of the meat is pierced with a knitting needle or skewer.

The authors of most cookbooks seem to find it necessary to specify the exact cooking time required for every ingredient in their recipes. We find this misleading, as so many different factors are involved in cooking over coals—not only the weight of the meat, fish, or vegetable, but also the thickness, cut, quality, length of time it has marinated, the way it was oiled, type of grill, temperature of the coals, distance from the coals, and so on. In short, we would need a computer to analyze all these factors and give a truly useful timing chart.

What we have done, therefore, is indicate in each recipe, for the specific size of piece we are using in that recipe, our recommended cooking time. Good taste and instinct, basic to this kind of cooking, will do the rest. As Brillat-Savarin, a brilliant gastronomic writer, wrote at the beginning of the last century, "You can learn to be a sauce chef, but roasting cooks are born."

ACCOMPANYING WINES

The French say things always end in song. I wonder if the source of this song is the excellent wines they drink. Certainly we should not present these recipes without some brief discussion of the wines that are best suited to barbecuing. The kind of food you are grilling should influence your choice of wine — you will undoubtedly choose different wines to accompany fish than you will to accompany meat.

As far as white wines are concerned, we recommend most highly the dry wines of the Loire valley: Muscadet, Gros-Plant, Sancerre, and Sauvignon. You might also enjoy whites from Savoy, Switzerland, the Jura, Alsatian Rieslings, and Tokays. Spanish whites to try are Vina Sol by Torres and those from the Rioja and Penedes regions, while good Italian whites are Soave by Bolla and Corva from Corsica. Try also the Californian Chardonnay, Sauvignon (particularly the fumée blanc), and Chablis and the Ontario Chardonnay (by Château des Charmes and Inniskillen), Riesling, and Gewürztraminer.

Of the rosés, which are a good accompaniment for lamb, vegetables, and some fish, we recommend Bandol, Tavel, Lirac, and in general the rosés from Provence and Corsica.

However, you will find that red wines are suited to the majority of barbecue recipes, and in general we prefer the French Beaujolais: Chiroubles, Juliénas, Saint-Amour, Morgon, Fleurie, and Brouilly; followed by the Loire reds: Bourgueil, Chinon, Saumur Champigny; or any other affordable wine that can be drunk cool. For a more grandiose barbecue you might wish to choose a Bordeaux, in which case a Graves or Saint-Émilion is good. If you prefer a Burgundy, we recommend a Côtes de Beaune or a Volnay. But Burgundys tend to be very expensive, so you might wish to choose from other French reds: Côtes du Ventoux, Côtes du Rhône le Velage, Châteauneuf-du-Pape, Crozes-Hermitage, Mâcon Rouge, and Bourgogne Pinot Noire.

Of the Spanish reds, the Riojas are particularly good, such as Brigadier Miranda, as is Torres Coronas from the Penedes region. We can also recommend the Portuguese Barriada from the Alianca region and Dao Reserva. There are lots of Italian reds to choose from — Chianti, especially Chianti Classico Riserva by Antinori, Valpolicella, and individual wines like Amarone by Negrar and Barolo by Fontanafredda. The Californian Cabernet Sauvignon wines are very good and vary in price, and the Zinfandels are generally less expensive; the Burgundies are also good. Recommended Ontario reds are Marechal Foch (by Inniskillen and Charal), Pinot Noir (by Château des Charmes), Bright's Baco Noir, and Andrés California Cellars Burgundy and Cabernet Sauvignon (made by Andrés's winemakers in California and imported).

HERBS, SPICES, AND CONDIMENTS USED IN BARBECUING

HERBS

Basil Finely shredded, on cooked chicken, fish, and lamb.

Bay Finely chopped or crumbled, sprinkled on meat before cooking.

Bouquet garni A little bundle of herbs, usually parsley, thyme, and bay leaf (stems tied together if fresh, knotted in a scrap of muslin if dried), to flavor marinades and sauces.

Chervil Used like parsley.

Dill Chopped, on salmon and trout.

Fennel Chopped, on white-fleshed fish: sea bass, red mullet, etc.

Marjoram Chopped, on grilled veal, pork, and fish.

Parsley Finely shredded, on all grilled foods and in all side salads.

Peppermint Finely shredded, on grilled lamb and some shellfish.

Rosemary Chopped, sparingly on grilled lamb, pork, and chicken.

Sage Finely shredded, on grilled pork.

Tarragon Finely shredded, on raw vegetables.

Thyme flowers Obtained by rubbing sprigs of fresh thyme between your hands over a plate. On all grilled foods.

SPICES

Cayenne A hot spice that doesn't spoil the flavor of food.

Cloves Whole, in marinades.

Coriander On organ meats, sausage, game, and poultry.

Curry powder On lamb and chicken cooked Indian style.

Ginger Ground, on lamb, beef, and chicken.

Juniper In marinades and cabbage-based salads.

Nutmeg For ground meat, especially chicken and veal.

Paprika Dusted on lamb and chicken before grilling.

Pepper (white, black, green) Whole, in marinades; ground or cracked, on grilled foods.

Saffron In fish marinades.

CONDIMENTS

Garlic Chopped, on fish, on lamb after grilling, and in many sauces and salads.

Lemon juice In nearly all marinades and most sauces and salads.

Onion Used like shallot, particularly in warm sauces.

Salt Often used only at the very last stage of cooking. Heightens all flavors. Indispensable. Can be replaced by dietetic salts for people on restricted diets.

Shallot Chopped, on fish, white meat, and beef. Used very much like garlic.

Sugar In some marinades, especially for game, and in sweet and sour sauces.

Vinegar (wine, white, cider, rice, champagne) A rival to lemon juice. Used in marinades and many sauces.

NOTES TO THE READER

You may notice that some of the ingredients given in this cookbook cannot be found in your particular part of the country or at certain times of the year, so in a number of cases we have suggested alternatives that might be more readily available. Sometimes a particular cut of meat specified in the French edition might be unobtainable, so we have substituted the closest equivalent that will be familiar to your butcher. In some recipes you may wish to make your own substitutions. We encourage you to use these recipes creatively and adapt them to your changing needs and developing culinary skills.

Although it is preferable to use fresh herbs, you can use dried herbs instead; generally, substitute one-third dried herbs for the amount of fresh herbs the recipe calls for. In most cases we list both the quantity of fresh and the equivalent of dried. Some of the terms used, like *a drop of* and *a dash of*, do not correspond to any exact measure but indicate that the ingredient should be used very sparingly to give only a hint of flavor. Please also note that the butter called for in these recipes is, unless otherwise specified, sweet or unsalted butter.

I
MARINADES

(Portions given are for 1.5 kg (scant 3 1/4 lb) of fish or meat.)

1. Marinade for Fish

250 ml (1 cup) olive oil
Juice of 1 lemon
Leaves from 2 sprigs fresh rosemary
1 tsp crushed cumin seeds *or* pinch ground
    cumin

Marinate for no longer than 1 hour.

2. Marinade for Fish
(variation)

6 tbsp olive oil
1 lime, peeled completely with a knife and
    sliced
Bouquet garni
1 stalk fresh fennel *or* 1 tbsp dried fennel
1 sprig fresh basil *or* 1 tbsp dried basil
1 onion, grated
1 shallot, finely chopped
Pinch curry powder
10 white peppercorns
Pinch salt

Marinate for no longer than 1 hour.

3. Marinade for Shellfish

6 tbsp olive oil
Juice of 1 lime
Pinch saffron
Fresh-ground white pepper

Marinate for no longer than 1 hour.

4. Marinade for Game and Poultry

3 tbsp cognac
120 ml (1/2 cup) red wine for game *or*
    white wine for poultry
1 onion, chopped
2 tbsp olive oil
1 tbsp fresh savory *or* 1 tsp dried savory
    (use thyme if savory isn't available)
White pepper

Marinate for 2 hours.

5. Marinade for Pork and Some Kinds of Poultry
(for pheasant, turkey, etc.)

30 ml (about 1 oz) cognac
2 tbsp olive oil
2 onions, finely chopped
1 clove garlic, crushed
Fresh-ground black pepper
1 tsp finely shredded fresh marjoram *or* pinch dried marjoram

Marinate for 2 hours.

6. Genghis Khan Marinade
(for grilled lamb)

2 tbsp sherry
1 tbsp soy sauce
2 tbsp finely chopped onion
2 tbsp olive oil
1 tbsp harissa sauce*
Fresh-ground white pepper

Marinate for 1 to 2 hours.

*The North African hot red pepper sauce usually served with couscous. This homemade substitute makes 5 tbsp. Pound 1/2 tsp seeded and chopped fresh chili to a paste in a mortar, keeping it as far from your face as possible. (Or substitute 1/2 tsp chili powder.) Add 1 tsp ground cumin, 1 tsp ground coriander, 1/2 tsp celery salt, and 2 tbsp tomato puree or tomato catsup. Then stir in 2 tbsp hot stock.

7. Marinade for Red Meat

200 ml (3/4 cup) red wine
5 tbsp wine vinegar
3 tbsp olive oil
4 tbsp chopped carrot, onion, shallot, and celery
Bouquet garni
2 tbsp cognac
1 clove garlic, peeled and crushed
2 cloves
6 black peppercorns
4 whole coriander seeds
Pinch salt

Marinate overnight.

II
COMPOUND BUTTERS

8. Smoked Salmon Butter
(for grilled salmon or trout)

Serves 4

100 g (3 1/2 oz) smoked salmon
100 g (3 1/2 oz) sweet butter, softened

Use a blender to finely chop the salmon;
then reduce it to a paste with a mortar and
pestle. Cream the butter. Add the smoked
salmon puree and mix until smooth and
creamy. Keep in a cool place.

9. Anchovy Butter
(for grilled fish)

Serves 4

100 g (3 1/2 oz) sweet butter, softened
2 tbsp anchovy paste

In a bowl cream the butter. Add the
anchovy paste. Beat until smooth. Keep in a
cool place.

10. Shallot Butter
(for freshwater fish and grilled red meat)

Serves 4

4 shallots
100 g (3 1/2 oz) sweet butter, softened
Salt, white pepper

Peel the shallots and blanch for 2 minutes in
salted, boiling water. Dry in a clean dish
towel, then crush thoroughly in a mortar.
Cream the butter. Blend in the shallots until
a smooth paste is formed. Season with salt
and pepper. Keep in a cool place.

11. Pistou* Butter
(for grilled meat and fish)

Serves 4

**2 cloves garlic, peeled
1 sprig fresh basil *or* 1 tbsp dried basil
100 g (3 1/2 oz) sweet butter, softened
Juice of half a lemon
Salt**

Crush the garlic and basil in a mortar. This gives you the pistou. Cream the butter and work it in, adding the lemon juice a few drops at a time. Salt lightly. Keep in a cool place.

   *Better known as *pesto*. This French version is made without nuts.

12. Tarragon Butter
(for grilled meat and fish)

Serves 4

**20 leaves fresh tarragon *or* 2 tbsp dried tarragon
50 g (1 3/4 oz) sweet butter, softened
50 g (1 3/4 oz) maître d'hôtel butter (Recipe 17)
Lemon juice (if required)**

Strip the tarragon leaves from their stems and crush them in a mortar. Work in the butter, then incorporate the maître d'hôtel butter. If the mixture is too stiff, add a few drops of lemon juice. Keep in a cool place.

13. Almond Butter
(for grilled white meat)

Serves 4

**75 g (2 3/4 oz) slivered almonds, lightly toasted
100 g (3 1/2 oz) sweet butter, softened
Salt, white pepper**

Crush the almonds in a mortar until very fine. (Sprinkle with a few drops of cool water so the oil does not separate.) Cream the butter and blend in the almond paste. Season with salt and pepper. Beat until completely smooth. Keep in a cool place.

14. Hazelnut Butter
(for grilled white meat)

Serves 4

**75 g (2 3/4 oz) hazelnuts, lightly toasted
100 g (3 1/2 oz) lightly salted butter, softened**

Crush the hazelnuts in a mortar until very fine. (Sprinkle with a few drops of cool water so the oil does not separate.) Cream the butter, then add the ground hazelnuts. Keep in a cool place.

15. Tomato Butter
(for grilled white meat)

Serves 4

4 tomatoes, peeled, seeded, and crushed
Sweet butter, softened
Salt, white pepper

Wring the tomatoes in a clean cloth to drain them. Blend the tomato pulp with an equal weight of butter. Season with salt and pepper. Keep in a cool place.

16. Combalou Butter
(for grilled meat)

Serves 4

100 g (3 1/2 oz) sweet butter, softened
Fresh parsley, chopped, *or* dried parsley
85 g (3 oz) Roquefort cheese
1 tbsp cognac
Fresh-ground white pepper

Cream the butter. Add the parsley. Crush the Roquefort with a fork and mash it until it forms a paste. Combine the butter and Roquefort paste. Add the cognac drop by drop. Season generously with pepper. Keep in a cool place.

17. Maître d'Hôtel Butter
(for grilled meat)

Serves 4

100 g (3 1/2 oz) sweet butter, softened
2 tbsp finely chopped parsley
Juice of half a lemon
Salt, white pepper

Cream the butter with a wooden spoon. (If you place the bowl on a damp cloth, it will be less likely to slip.) Add the parsley, lemon juice, salt, and pepper. Blend well. Set aside in a cool place for at least 1 hour.

III
Sauces

COLD SAUCES

18. Sauce Troisgros
(for grilled fish)

Serves 4

2 egg yolks
1 tsp Dijon mustard
Pinch salt
Juice of 1 lemon
180 ml (3/4 cup) peanut oil
1 shallot, very finely chopped
Few drops Tabasco sauce
Leaves of 3 sprigs watercress, finely
  shredded

In a mixing bowl whisk the egg yolks,
mustard, salt, and a third of the lemon juice.
Add the oil drop by drop, whisking briskly
and continuously. Add the remaining lemon
juice, then the shallot, Tabasco sauce, and
watercress.

19. Red Pepper Sauce
(for grilled red mullet)

Serves 4

Mullet entrails
1 tbsp sweet butter, softened
1 tbsp lemon juice
2 pinches salt
10–12 dried hot red pepper seeds, crushed
150 ml (2/3 cup) olive oil

Empty the entrails from the grilled mullet
into a bowl. With a small whisk blend in the
butter, then the lemon juice, salt, and hot
pepper seeds. Add the oil drop by drop,
beating continuously.

20. Pepper Sauce
(for white meat)

Serves 4

4 green peppers
100 ml (1/3 cup) red wine
2 tbsp paprika
Salt, fresh-ground white pepper

Remove the seeds from the peppers; slice
them and put them through a blender. Make
a dressing with the red wine, paprika, salt,
and pepper. Add the dressing to the pepper
puree and mix well.

MAYONNAISES

(for all grilled meat and fish)

Basic Mayonnaise

1 egg yolk
Equal volume hot *or* spicy mustard
180 ml (3/4 cup) olive, peanut, *or*
**   sunflower oil**
2 tbsp wine or cider vinegar *or* lemon juice
Salt, pepper

Allow the ingredients to reach room
temperature. Beat the egg yolk and mustard
together. When the mixture is smooth, beat
in the oil drop by drop, always stirring in
the same direction, until the mixture is
thick. Season with salt and pepper. Add the
vinegar or lemon juice. Let stand in a cool
place.

Tips on Making a Good Mayonnaise

1. It is important for the ingredients to be at
    room temperature. About 2 hours before
    you intend to make the sauce, set aside
    the ingredients—egg yolk, mustard, oil,
    lemon juice or vinegar—and your mixing
    bowl in a corner of the kitchen.

2. If you have to use an egg straight from
    the refrigerator, separate the yolk from
    the white, mix the yolk with an equal
    volume of mustard, beat well, and set
    aside for 10 minutes. The mustard will
    "warm" the egg yolk.
3. To make the mayonnaise lighter: after it
    is prepared, rapidly beat in 2 tbsp
    almost-boiling water.
4. If at any point the mayonnaise threatens
    to curdle, quickly add 2 tbsp almost-
    boiling water. This usually solves the
    problem. If not, beat a second egg yolk
    with an equal volume of mustard and
    add the first mixture very slowly and
    carefully to this new base.

21. Aïoli

To 250 ml (1 cup) basic mayonnaise add
4 cloves crushed garlic. Season generously
with salt and pepper to taste. This is a simple
and practical modification of the classic aïoli
recipe.

22. Scottish

To 250 ml (1 cup) basic mayonnaise add
3 tbsp catsup and 1 tsp Scotch whisky. Season
generously with salt and cayenne pepper to
taste.

23. Green

To 250 ml (1 cup) basic mayonnaise add
3 tbsp of a mixture of chopped fresh
parsley, chervil, chives, and tarragon or
3 tsp of the same herbs, dried. Season
generously with salt and pepper to taste.

24. Tartare

To 250 ml (1 cup) basic mayonnaise add a
mixture of 2 large sour gherkins and 1 tbsp
capers, both finely chopped. Season
generously with salt and pepper to taste.

25. Portuguese

To 250 ml (1 cup) basic mayonnaise add 1/2
can flat anchovy fillets, drained and mashed.
Season with salt and pepper to taste.

26. Caribbean

To 2 tbsp basic mayonnaise add the flesh of
1 small avocado put through a blender with
the juice of 1 lemon. Season generously
with salt, white pepper, and ginger to taste.

27. Acapulco

To 250 ml (1 cup) basic mayonnaise add
1 small hot pepper, finely chopped, 1 tsp
paprika, 1 pinch saffron, and 1 dash tequila
(optional). Season generously with salt to
taste.

28. Mustard

To 250 ml (1 cup) basic mayonnaise add
2 tbsp *crème fraîche** and 3 tbsp prepared
hot mustard.

* A slightly sharp cream often used in
cuisine minceur as a substitute for thick
cream in many savory recipes. Here is a
recipe that makes 450 ml (a little less than
2 cups).
    Combine 300 ml (1 1/3 cups) thick
cream *or* 35% cream, such as whipping
cream, and 150 ml (2/3 cup) buttermilk
or sour cream in a heavy-based saucepan
and heat gently to 32°C (90°F); at this
temperature it will still feel slightly cool
to the touch. Pour into a bowl, cover, and
leave to thicken in a warm place for 8
hours. Stir well, then chill before using. It
will keep, covered, in the refrigerator for
about 1 week. As a substitute for *crème
fraîche* you can use 35% cream, such as
whipping cream.

SAUCES FOR GRILLED BEEF

29. Gherkins with Cream

Rinse some sour pickled gherkins. Chop finely and mix with thick cream.* Use 1 tbsp chopped gherkins to 2 tbsp cream.

 *A number of recipes in this cookbook call for thick cream. If you have no source for the French *crème épaisse*, we suggest you substitute heavy (35%) cream, such as whipping cream.

30. Bulgarian Pearl Onions

Beat together equal amounts of well-drained cottage cheese and yogurt. The mixture should have a firm consistency. Rinse the pickled onions well, chop finely, and add to the cheese/yogurt mixture. Use 1 tbsp chopped onions to 2 tbsp cheese/yogurt mixture.

31. Puszta Mayonnaise

Add 2 tbsp well-rinsed, chopped capers to 8 tbsp mayonnaise made with olive oil. Season with Hungarian paprika until the sauce becomes deep orange.

32. Crème Niçoise

Mash some pitted, fresh black olives to a paste in a mortar. Blend with thick cream *or* 35% cream, such as whipping cream: 1 part olive paste to 3 parts cream.

Note: Olives preserved in vinegar will curdle the cream.

33. Cream Sauce with Herbs

Chop a mixture of fresh tarragon and fresh basil (or dried herbs if fresh ones aren't available). Beat together 2 tbsp thick cream *or* 35% cream, such as whipping cream, and 4 tbsp *petit suisse** cheese; add the herbs.

   *A fresh, very creamy French cheese sold in small cartons. Often mixed with sugar or pepper.

34. Egg Sauce

Make a runny ''omelet'' with 2 eggs and a little tomato paste diluted with water. Work the mixture into a paste and mix it with an equal amount of thick cream *or* 35% cream, such as whipping cream. Flavor with 2 pinches cayenne. Season with salt to taste.

35. Madagascar Sauce

In a mortar grind 4 tbsp green peppercorns. Add 1 egg yolk and the juice of half a lime. Beat well and add thick cream *or* 35% cream, such as whipping cream, until a thick sauce is formed.

WARM SAUCES

36. White Port Sauce
(for grilled fish)

Serves 4

100 g (3 1/2 oz) butter, softened
1 tbsp anchovy paste
1 tbsp white port
Fresh-ground white pepper
Juice of half a lime

In a bowl cream the butter. Blend in the anchovy paste and port to lighten the mixture. Turn into a thick-bottomed saucepan and bring slowly to a boil, stirring continuously with a wooden spoon.

Remove from the grill, season generously with pepper, and add the lime juice. Keep warm.

37. Shallot Sauce
(for grilled fish)

Serves 6

4 chopped shallots
175 g (6 oz) butter
1 tbsp finely shredded fresh parsley *or*
  1 tsp dried parsley
Yolks of 4 hard-boiled eggs, mashed with a
  fork
Juice of 1 lemon
Salt, white pepper

In a thick-bottomed, covered saucepan cook the shallots gently in 1 tbsp butter. Remove from the pan and set aside.

In the same pan melt the remaining butter. Remove from the grill. Add the parsley, egg yolk paste, lemon juice, salt, and pepper. Mix well with a wooden spoon. Finally, add the shallots. Keep warm.

38. Sauce Bercy
(for grilled fish)

Serves 4

3 shallots, very finely chopped
150 g (5 oz) butter
200 ml (3/4 cup) dry white wine
Juice of half a lemon
Salt, white pepper
Fresh parsley, finely shredded

In a thick-bottomed, covered saucepan
gently braise the shallots in 2 tbsp butter.
Add the white wine and cook until the sauce
is reduced to two-thirds. Remove from the
grill and whip in the lemon juice, salt,
and pepper.

Still whipping, blend in the remaining
butter, adding it in small chunks. The sauce
will expand like a smooth mayonnaise.
Keep warm. Sprinkle with chopped parsley
just before serving.

39. Sauce Diable
(for grilled organ meats and poultry)

Serves 4

4 tbsp red wine vinegar
3 shallots, chopped
4 tbsp tomato puree
50 g (1 3/4 oz) butter
Salt, fresh-ground white pepper

Put the vinegar and shallots into a
thick-bottomed, covered saucepan. Cook
until the liquid is reduced to half. Add the
tomato puree and boil for 2 minutes.
Remove from the barbecue and stir in the
butter. Season with salt and a generous
amount of pepper. Keep warm.

40. Sauce Chasseur
(for grilled white meat and poultry)

Serves 4

50 g (1 3/4 oz) sweet butter
100 g (3 1/2 oz) white mushrooms, minced
1 shallot, chopped
60 ml (1/4 cup) dry white wine
Salt, white pepper
5 tbsp tomato puree
1 tsp each finely shredded fresh tarragon
**   and chervil**

Melt 1 tbsp butter in a pan, add the
mushrooms, and cook gently for 2 minutes.
Add the shallot and continue to cook
2 minutes longer, stirring continuously. Stir
in the wine and cook until the liquid is
reduced to half. Season with salt and
pepper. Add the tomato puree and boil for
2 minutes.

Remove from the grill. With a wooden
spoon stir in the remaining butter. Keep
warm. Sprinkle with the fresh, chopped
herbs just before serving.

41. Sauce Duxelles
(for grilled ham and white meat)

Serves 4

75 g (2 3/4 oz) butter
3 shallots, chopped
100 g (3 1/2 oz) mushrooms, chopped
120 ml (1/2 cup) dry white wine
300 ml (1 1/4 cup) chicken stock
2 tbsp tomato puree
Fresh-ground white pepper
Fresh parsley, finely shredded

In a thick-bottomed pan melt 1 tbsp butter, add the shallots, and cook until golden. Add the mushrooms and cook, stirring with a wooden spoon, until they release their liquid. Add the wine and cook until the liquid has evaporated.

Add the tomato puree to the chicken stock and pour this mixture into the saucepan. Cook until it is reduced to two-thirds. Remove from the grill and add the remaining butter. Season with pepper. Keep warm. Sprinkle with shredded parsley before serving.

42. Pork Butcher's Sauce
(for grilled pork, poultry, calf's liver, and other organ meats)

Serves 4

2 tbsp dry white wine
2 tbsp white wine vinegar
2 shallots, chopped
60 ml (1/4 cup) chicken stock
1 tbsp chopped sour gherkins
Fresh-ground white pepper
1 tsp each finely shredded fresh parsley, chervil, and tarragon

Pour the wine and vinegar into a thick-bottomed pan, add the shallots, and cook until the liquid is reduced to half. Add the stock and cook for 5 more minutes.

Remove from the grill. Add the gherkins and season with pepper. Keep warm. Sprinkle with chopped herbs before serving.

43. Yorkshire Sauce
(for grilled pork and spit-roasted game birds)

Serves 4

120 ml (1/2 cup) port
Zest* of 1 orange, very finely minced
2 tbsp tomato puree
1 tsp bilberry *or* cranberry jelly
Pinch powdered cinnamon
Fresh-ground white pepper, salt
4 tbsp fresh orange juice

Cook the zest in the port for 5 minutes. Strain and reserve the cooked zest. Return the port to the saucepan and add the tomato puree, bilberry or cranberry jelly, and cinnamon. Season generously with pepper. Salt to taste. Cook for 2 minutes.

Strain the sauce through a sieve into another saucepan and stir in the fresh orange juice and orange zest. Keep warm.

*Zest is the colored and aromatic outer layer of the peel of citrus fruits.

44. Sauce Robert
(for grilled or spit-roasted pork)

Serves 6

300 g (10 oz) onions
1 tbsp butter
Flour
400 ml (1 3/4 cups) veal *or* beef stock
400 ml (1 3/4 cups) dry white wine
Salt, white pepper
1 tbsp prepared hot mustard

Dice the onions. Sauté them in the butter in a thick-bottomed saucepan until they are golden. Sprinkle with a little flour and cook for 2 minutes more, stirring continuously. Pour in the stock and wine. Season with salt and pepper. Simmer for 10 minutes, stirring from time to time.

Remove from the grill and add the mustard. Do not cook any longer. If you are roasting the pork on a spit, add the drippings to the sauce. Keep warm.

45. Fresh Tomato Sauce
(for grilled lamb)

4 tomatoes
2 tbsp butter
1 onion, chopped
Salt
Pinch cayenne pepper
100 ml (1/3 cup) tomato paste
Fresh parsley, chopped, *or* dried parsley

Scald the tomatoes; peel, seed, and crush them.

On a corner of the barbecue in a small saucepan melt 1 tbsp butter and sauté the onion until golden. Season with salt and cayenne. Add the tomato paste and bring to a boil. Remove from the grill and beat in the remaining butter, a little at a time. Sprinkle with parsley.

46. Mint Sauce
(for grilled lamb)

Serves 8

1 bunch fresh mint *or* 2 tbsp dried mint
Fresh-ground white pepper
25 ml (scant 1 oz) sugar
50 ml (scant 1/4 cup) stock
120 ml (1/2 cup) white wine vinegar

If using fresh mint, pick the leaves from the stems, wash, dry in a clean dish towel, then chop very finely. Put into a small bowl with the pepper and sugar.

Bring the stock and vinegar to a boil and pour over the mint mixture. Cover and leave to infuse for at least 1 hour. Reheat the sauce before serving.

47. Sauce Bouzy
(for red meat)

Serves 6

1/2 bottle Bouzy *or* any good red wine
2 shallots, chopped
1 bay leaf
1 tbsp thyme flowers *or* 1 tsp dried thyme
Fresh-ground white pepper
100 g (3 1/2 oz) butter
Salt

Pour the wine into a thick-bottomed saucepan. Add the shallots, bay leaf, thyme, and pepper. Cook until the liquid is reduced to one-quarter. Add the juice from carving the meat. Remove the bay leaf. Over low heat stir in the butter. Season with salt to taste. Serve very hot, poured over the meat.

IV
APPETIZERS AND GARNISHES

48. Scallops Sevruga

Serves 4

16 large scallops
6 tbsp hazelnut or peanut oil
Juice of 1 lemon
Salt, fresh-ground white pepper
60 g (2 oz) Sevruga *or* salmon *or* lumpfish caviar

With a very sharp knife cut each scallop into 3 horizontal slices. In a bowl beat together the hazelnut or peanut oil and lemon juice. Dip the scallops into this dressing and wipe off the excess with a brush.

Arrange the scallops on 4 well-chilled plates and season them very lightly with salt and pepper. Arrange the caviar in the middle of each slice. Serve cold.

49. Blaze of Shellfish

Selection of your favorite shellfish
Plenty of dry straw mixed with dry pine needles
Fresh-ground white pepper
Fresh whole wheat bread
Lightly salted butter

Arrange the shellfish in a single layer on the grill of an unlit barbecue (or on the sand if you are at the beach). Cover them with half the straw/pine needles mixture and set fire to it. Repeat. Fan the remaining embers. Use a kitchen bellows if you have them. The heat will open the shellfish. Season with pepper and eat immediately with fresh bread and butter.

50. Ceviche Polynesian Style

Serves 6

1 kg (2 1/4 lb) fillets very fresh fish (for
    example, hake, haddock, cod)
Juice of 8 limes
Salt, white pepper
200 ml (3/4 cup) coconut milk (available in
    fine food stores)
Good pinch cayenne pepper
200 ml (3/4 cup) light (15%) cream
1 tsp each fresh chervil, chives, and
    tarragon, shredded with scissors

Cut the fish into 1.5-cm (just over 1/2″)
cubes. Marinate in the lime juice for 2 hours,
covered and in a cool place.

    Drain the fish and pat very gently dry.
Spread the pieces on a deep platter and
season with salt and pepper. Beat the
coconut milk lightly with the cayenne.
Repeat for the cream. Pour both onto the
fish. Mix well.

    Keep in a cool place until just before
serving, then garnish with the shredded
herbs.

Note: Do not attempt this ceviche with any
but the freshest fish. Never use frozen fish.

51. Anchoïade

5 cloves garlic, peeled
200 g (7 oz) anchovy paste
1 small glass (about 1 1/2 oz) olive oil
Juice of 1 lemon
Fresh-ground white pepper
Raw vegetables to dip in the anchoïade:
    celery sticks
    tomatoes cut into wedges
    small, tender purple artichokes
      (optional)
    florets of cauliflower or broccoli
    hearts of fennel
    radishes
    etc.

Crush the garlic. Add the anchovy paste,
then drop by drop the oil, followed by the
lemon juice. Season generously with
pepper. Serve as a dip with a selection of
raw vegetables and with slices of bread
lightly toasted over the barbecue and
rubbed with garlic.

52. Eggs en Brochettes

Serves 4

8 large, very fresh eggs
Salt, fresh-ground white pepper
3 tbsp butter
20 leaves fresh sage, finely chopped,
    ***or* 2 tbsp dried sage**
2 leaves fresh mint, finely chopped,
    ***or* 2 tsp dried mint**
Large syringe *or* pastry tube with a very
    fine nozzle

Over a mixing bowl puncture the eggs at
each end with a large needle. Blow through
one of the holes to empty them into the
bowl. Set the empty shells carefully aside.
Beat the eggs; add the salt and pepper. Melt
the butter in a pan. Add the eggs and cook
lightly; they should not quite set. Remove
from the heat and add the herbs.

Divide the egg mixture into 8 equal
portions and, using a large syringe, fill the
eggshells with the omelet. Thread 2 eggs
onto each skewer and grill for 5 minutes
over the barbecue, turning once. Serve the
eggs on the skewer.

53. Baba Ghannouj

Serves 4

4 small eggplants (the long, narrow kind)
    ***or* 1 large one**
8 cloves garlic, peeled
Salt, fresh-ground white pepper
4 tbsp chopped fresh parsley *or* 4 tsp dried
    parsley
Juice of half a lemon
Olive oil

Grill the eggplants. When the skins are crisp
and crackled all over, immerse them in cold
water for 3 minutes, then peel them with
your hands under running water. Chop
them very finely, using a large kitchen knife.

Mash the garlic thoroughly in a mortar
and add to the chopped eggplant. Season
generously with salt and pepper, then add
the parsley and lemon juice. Mix well. With
a small whisk add the oil drop by drop to
the eggplant mixture, which will expand
like a mayonnaise. Continue to add oil as
long as the eggplant puree will absorb it.
Serve cool with pieces of crusty bread
rubbed with garlic and sprinkled with a few
drops of olive oil.

54. Medley of Artichoke Hearts

Serves 6

**6 large artichoke hearts, blanched and
  diced
150 g (5 oz) roast chicken, diced
150 g (5 oz) pickled tongue, diced
150 g (5 oz) well-cured ham, diced
1/2 bunch watercress
1 tbsp grated fresh horseradish
200 ml (3/4 cup) mustard mayonnaise
  (Recipe 28)
2 hard-boiled eggs, sliced
1 tsp each fresh chervil and tarragon,
  shredded with scissors**

In a large, chilled salad bowl mix together
the artichoke hearts, chicken, tongue, and
ham. Add the watercress, horseradish, and
mustard mayonnaise. Mix. Garnish with the
hard-boiled eggs sprinkled with the herbs.
Serve cool.

55. Tabouleh

Serves 4

**200 g (7 oz) precooked, dry bulgur *or*
  cracked wheat *or* large-grain couscous
Lettuce leaves
Juice of 4 lemons
4 tomatoes, peeled, seeded, and diced
3 green onions, chopped
1 bunch fresh mint, shredded with scissors
4 tbsp chopped fresh parsley *or* 4 tsp dried
  parsley
200 ml (3/4 cup) olive oil
Salt, white pepper**

Wrap the bulgur in muslin, knot loosely, and
place in a deep bowl. Cover with cold water
and leave to swell for 1 hour. In the
meantime line a large salad bowl with
lettuce leaves.

  Remove the bulgur from the water and
wring out as much water as possible.
Discard the water, empty the bulgur back
into the bowl, and mix in the lemon juice.
Add the tomatoes, onions, mint, and
parsley. Pour in the oil and season with salt
and pepper. Mix well. Arrange in the salad
bowl and serve cool.

56. Leeks with Lemon

Serves 4

6 leeks
1 tbsp olive oil
Salt, white pepper
Lemon juice

Remove the green from the leeks. Partly split the whites lengthwise, but do not separate them. Wash thoroughly. Put into a heavy, covered casserole with the oil. Add salt and pepper. Cover and cook for 15 minutes on a corner of the barbecue. At the end of this time the leeks will have browned evenly. Sprinkle with lemon juice, re-cover, and cook very gently for a further 40 minutes.

This dish is a perfect accompaniment for grilled veal.

57. Mechouiya

Serves 6

6 tomatoes
3 green bell peppers
Pinch salt
3 tbsp vinegar
Juice of 1 lemon
6 tbsp olive oil
Fresh-ground white pepper
2 cloves garlic, minced or finely mashed
1 can flaked tuna in oil, drained
3 hard-boiled eggs, cut into wedges
Green and black olives, pitted

Grill the tomatoes and peppers quickly over a very hot fire. Peel and seed them and cut into very thin strips. Arrange on a chilled serving platter.

Prepare the vinaigrette by mixing the salt with the vinegar, then adding the lemon juice, oil, pepper, and garlic. Pour the vinaigrette over the grilled vegetables and add the tuna. Mix well. Garnish with the hard-boiled eggs and green and black olives. Chill for at least 1 hour before serving.

V

SALADS

58. Lettuce with Cream

Serves 4

1 firm head lettuce
3 tbsp thick cream *or* 35% cream, such as
**   whipping cream**
1 tbsp lemon juice
Salt, white pepper

Wash the lettuce and dry in a clean dish
towel. Cut into strips. Mix the cream, lemon
juice, salt, and pepper in a large bowl.
Add the lettuce, mix well, and serve
immediately.

Variation: Use the hearts of 4 romaine
lettuces instead of head lettuce.

59. Lettuce with Roquefort

Serves 4

1 firm head lettuce
150 g (5 oz) Roquefort cheese
Pinch salt
1 tbsp vinegar
3 tbsp peanut oil
1 clove garlic, minced or finely mashed
White pepper
1 tbsp fresh chervil, chives, and parsley,
**   shredded with scissors, *or* 1 tsp of the**
**   same herbs, dried**

Remove damaged leaves from the lettuce.
Wash the lettuce and dry in a clean dish
towel. With a fork crumble the Roquefort.
    Prepare the vinaigrette in a salad bowl.
Mix the salt with the vinegar, then add the
oil, garlic, pepper, and herbs. Put the lettuce
in the bowl and sprinkle with the crumbled
cheese. Mix just before serving.

60. Wild Salad Greens Dauphin

Serves 4

**250 g (8 oz) lamb's lettuce (*or* any wild
  greens in season: dandelion greens,
  lamb's quarters, etc.) *or* spinach, beet
  greens, *or* very young kale
1 choice eating apple
Juice of 1 lemon
1 clove garlic, minced or finely mashed
12 green walnuts
12 black olives, pitted
2 tbsp peanut oil
1 tbsp walnut oil
1 tbsp tarragon vinegar
Salt, white pepper**

Carefully wash the greens several times and
dry in a clean dish towel. Peel and dice the
apple and sprinkle with lemon juice so it
doesn't turn brown. In a large bowl mix the
lettuce, diced apple, garlic, walnuts, and
olives.

   In another bowl beat together the oils and
the vinegar. Season with salt and pepper.
Pour the vinaigrette over the salad just
before serving. Mix well.

61. Dandelion Greens with Bacon

Serves 4

**400 g (14 oz) dandelion greens
200 g (7 oz) streaky bacon
Fresh-ground white pepper
2 tbsp red wine vinegar**

Wash the dandelion greens carefully several
times and dry in a clean dish towel. Brown
the bacon in a very hot frying pan. Pour the
entire contents of the frying pan into a
heated serving bowl and pepper generously.
Rinse the vinegar quickly over the hot
frying pan and pour into the dressing. Add
the dandelion greens. Mix and serve
immediately.

Variation: Use finely shredded red cabbage
instead of dandelion greens.

62. Celery Salad

Serves 4

2 heads celery
4 hard-boiled eggs
1 tsp prepared hot mustard
6 tbsp peanut oil
2 tbsp vinegar
Salt, white pepper
2 tbsp fresh chervil, tarragon, and chives,
** shredded with scissors**

Break off the stalks of the celery and remove the tough fibers at the base. Cut into chunks and blanch for 2 minutes in boiling, salted water. Drain and allow to cool.

In a salad bowl mash the egg yolks with a fork. Beat in the mustard, oil, vinegar, salt, and pepper. Finally, mince the egg whites finely and add to this mixture. Add the celery, which should still be a little warm. Mix well and allow to cool completely. Sprinkle with the herbs just before serving.

Variation: Use endive instead of celery. (It does not need blanching.)

63. Green Bean Salad

Serves 4

1 kg (2 1/4 lb) green string beans
Pinch salt
20 ml (3/4 oz) white wine vinegar
60 ml (1/4 cup) olive oil
1 clove garlic, minced
1 shallot, minced
1 red pepper, cut into thin rings

String the beans and throw them into a large pot of boiling, salted water. Cook at full boil with the lid off for 5 minutes if the beans are very fresh, 10 minutes if they are not. They should be cooked *al dente*. Remove from the pot with a slotted spoon and plunge immediately into cold water so that they keep almost all their color. Pat dry thoroughly with a paper towel.

In a large salad bowl prepare the dressing. Mix the salt with the vinegar, then add the oil, garlic, and shallot. Add the beans and pepper rings. Mix well. Keep in a cool place until served.

64. Broccoli Salad

Serves 4

1 kg (2 1/4 lb) broccoli
Pinch salt
2 tbsp vinegar
6 tbsp olive oil
1 clove garlic, minced
Pinch dried oregano

Break the broccoli into individual florets. Blanch for 2 minutes in boiling, salted water. Drain well and allow to cool.

Prepare the dressing in a salad bowl. Dissolve the salt in the vinegar, then add the oil, garlic, and oregano. Add the cooled broccoli, mix carefully, cover, and refrigerate for 1 hour before serving.

65. Grilled Tomato and Pepper Salad

Serves 4

2 large green bell peppers
4 firm tomatoes
3 tbsp olive oil
1 tbsp vinegar
Salt, white pepper
2 cloves garlic, chopped
2 tbsp fresh parsley, shredded with
    scissors, *or* 2 tsp dried parsley

Grill the peppers over the barbecue for 15 minutes, turning often. Stem the tomatoes and place them on the barbecue 6 minutes before the peppers are ready. Grill for 3 minutes on each side. Peel the peppers and tomatoes. Remove the seeds from the peppers and slice them. Cut the tomatoes into quarters over your salad bowl so none of the juice is lost.

Prepare the vinaigrette in the salad bowl. Mix the oil, vinegar, salt, and pepper, then add the garlic and parsley. Finally, add the vegetables and mix very carefully.

66. Mushroom Salad

Serves 4

500 g (generous 1 lb) mushrooms
Juice of 1 lemon
4 tbsp olive oil
Salt, white pepper

Wipe the mushrooms. If they have to be washed, dry them immediately in a clean dish towel. Slice into a salad bowl. Sprinkle with the lemon juice and mix. Add the olive oil, salt, and pepper. Mix, cover, and refrigerate for 1 hour before serving, stirring from time to time.

67. Potato Salad

Serves 4

4 large, firm potatoes
4 shallots, chopped
120 ml (1/2 cup) dry white wine
1 tbsp prepared hot mustard
Salt
2 tbsp white wine vinegar
6 tbsp oil
White pepper

Wrap each potato in aluminum foil. Place on
the barbecue and cook over a hot fire for
about 1 hour, turning once. Peel while still
hot and cut up into a salad bowl. Add the
shallots and pour the wine over
immediately. Cover and leave to soak
while you prepare the vinaigrette.

In another bowl mix the mustard, salt,
and vinegar, then add the oil; pepper to
taste. Pour the vinaigrette over the potatoes
and shallots and mix very carefully. Serve
warm or cold.

68. Salade Périgord*

Serves 4

4 medium-sized truffles, well brushed
8 very small artichokes *or* **8 artichoke**
 hearts *or* **8 florets of cauliflower**
Coarse salt
Yolks of 3 hard-boiled eggs
1 tsp prepared hot mustard
6 tbsp peanut oil
2 tbsp tarragon vinegar
Salt, white pepper
1 clove garlic, peeled

Slice the truffles very thinly. Split the
artichokes through the center and slice
them very thinly. Sprinkle with coarse salt
and let stand for 10 minutes, then dry in a
clean dish towel.

In a bowl mash the egg yolks with a fork.
A little at a time incorporate the mustard,
oil, vinegar, and a little salt and pepper.

Rub the bottom of a salad bowl with the
garlic clove, then arrange in thin, alternate
layers the truffles, artichokes, and a little of
the egg sauce. Allow to stand for 10
minutes, then mix very gently.

*Only in Périgord are truffles part of
 ordinary cuisine; the best black truffles
 grow in the oak forests of this southwestern
 French province. The *périgourdins* train
 their pigs to sniff the truffles out, then
 carry them home to dine like millionaires.

69. "Real" Salade Niçoise

Serves 6

4 tomatoes
1 English cucumber
Coarse salt
2 hard-boiled eggs
2 onions
1 green bell pepper
1 200 g (7 oz) can tuna in oil, drained
1 small can flat fillets of anchovy in oil
1 clove garlic, peeled
20 black olives
Salt
2 tbsp vinegar
6 tbsp olive oil
Generous amount fresh-ground pepper
Fresh or dried basil, shredded with
**   scissors**

Cut the tomatoes into quarters. Slice the cucumber very thinly, sprinkle with coarse salt, and let stand for 30 minutes. Do not peel the cucumber — you will digest it better this way. Cut the eggs into quarters and slice the onions very thinly. Grill the pepper on the barbecue, rub off the charred skin, remove the stem and seeds, and cut into thin rings. Crush the tuna with a fork and chop the anchovies into small pieces.

Rub the entire inside of a large salad bowl with a clove of garlic. Arrange in alternate layers the tomatoes, cucumber, eggs, onions, pepper, anchovies, tuna, and black olives. In another dish prepare the dressing by beating together the salt, vinegar, oil, and pepper. Sprinkle with basil. Pour the seasoning over the vegetables. Keep cool until served.

VI

FROM THE GRILL

FISH AND SEAFOOD

70. Grilled Eel with Sage

Serves 4

2 eels, each 500 g (generous 1 lb), without the heads
4 tbsp olive oil
40 leaves fresh sage, coarsely chopped, or 4 tbsp dried sage
4 leaves fresh mint or pinch dried mint
Salt, white pepper
200 ml (3/4 cup) thick cream or 35% cream, such as whipping cream
Juice of 1 lemon
3 tbsp fresh parsley, shredded with scissors, or 3 tsp dried parsley

Cut the eels into pieces about 8 cm (3″) long. With a very sharp knife make shallow slashes in the skin. Marinate for 24 hours in a mixture of the oil, sage, and mint. Turn frequently.

Grill gently on the barbecue for 20 minutes. Turn from time to time and baste with marinade. Transfer to a serving dish. Remove the skin (which will have protected the flesh during cooking). Season with salt and pepper. Serve with thick cream beaten with the lemon juice, salt, pepper, and parsley.

71. Grilled Pike Steaks

Serves 4

8 pike steaks, about 2 cm (about 3/4″) thick
200 ml (3/4 cup) olive oil
Juice of 1 lemon
Fresh parsley sprigs or 1 tbsp dried parsley
4 shallots, minced or very thinly sliced
Salt, white pepper
1 egg, beaten
Breadcrumbs
Melted butter

Marinate the steaks for 2 hours in the oil, lemon juice, parsley, shallots, salt, and pepper. Keep covered and in a cool place.

Remove from the marinade and dry with a clean dish towel. Dip in the egg, then in breadcrumbs. Place on a very hot, oiled grill. Cook for 2 minutes on each side. Turn very carefully with a spatula so they do not break. Sprinkle with melted butter before serving.

72. Grilled Salmon with Dill

Serves 4

**4 tbsp chopped fresh dill leaves *or* 4 tsp
  dried dill
100 g (3 1/2 oz) butter, softened
4 thick slices fresh salmon
Salt, white pepper
Oil**

Mash the dill in a mortar. Add the butter and
work the mixture until smooth. Set aside in
a cool place.

Season the salmon steaks with salt and
pepper. Brush with oil. Grill for 2 minutes,
give them a quarter turn, and grill 3 minutes
longer. Repeat on the other side. Serve with
a knob of dill butter on each.

73. Salmon Grilled on One Side

Serves 4

**4 fillets freshly caught salmon, with the
  skin on
Salt, white pepper**

This one-sided method of cooking provides
an intriguing gradation of flavors and
textures, from grilled to raw, and keeps the
fish very moist.

Place the salmon skin side down on the
grill and don't turn it. Remove from the grill
when all except the top 1 cm (3/8'') is
cooked. Season with salt and pepper. Eat
immediately without any sauce or garnish.

74. Barbecued Trout

Serves 4

**4 trout, cleaned but whole, *or* 750 g
  (1 1/2 lb) fillet of other fish, with the
  skin on
Salt
Oil**

Salt the trout 30 minutes before grilling or, if
you are serving fillets, 2 hours before. Heat
and lightly oil the grill. Cook the trout for
5 minutes on each side. Turn with a spatula.
Serve immediately. Grill fillets for 5 minutes
with the skin side toward the flame.

75. Grilled Cod

Serves 4

**4 cod steaks, about 4 cm (1 1/2'') thick
Salt, white pepper
Flour
Butter, melted
4 pinches celery seed *or* cumin seed *or*
  pinch dried cumin
Lemon wedges**

Season the steaks with salt and pepper and
dip in flour. Tap gently to get rid of excess
flour. Moisten with melted butter and grill
gently for 5 minutes on each side. Turn
gently with a spatula or use a hinged double
grill. Sprinkle each grilled steak with a pinch
of celery seed. Garnish with lemon wedges.

76. Grilled Shad with Sorrel Puree

Serves 4

4 large fillets shad *or* sea bass *or* fresh cod
2 cloves garlic, halved
4 tbsp peanut oil
Juice of 1 lemon
1 tbsp chopped fresh parsley *or* 1 tsp dried
**   parsley**
Thyme
Fresh or dried bay leaf, chopped
Salt, white pepper
600 g (generous 1 1/4 lb) homemade sorrel
**   puree***
Lemon wedges

Press half a clove of garlic into each fillet. In a mixing bowl prepare a marinade with the oil, lemon juice, parsley, thyme, bay leaf, salt, and pepper. Marinate the fish for about 20 minutes.

Dry the fish well and place on a hot grill. Cook for 6 minutes on each side, turning carefully with a spatula. Arrange the cooked shad on a bed of warm sorrel puree. Serve immediately, garnished with lemon wedges.

*Here is a recipe for sorrel puree. Put 1 kg (2 1/4 lb) sorrel, picked over and rinsed several times, into a big saucepan. Moisten with 3 tbsp water and cook over low heat until it goes down in volume. Drain in a sieve.

Prepare a blond roux made of 4 tbsp (1/4 cup) butter and 2 tbsp flour. Mix well, add 2 1/2 cups white stock, season with salt and a little castor sugar, cover the pan, and cook in the oven for 2 hours.

Rub the sorrel through a fine sieve and put it back in the pan to reheat. Bind with a liaison of 3 whole eggs (or 6 yolks), beaten, mixed with 6 tbsp (scant 1/2 cup) cream, strained and blended with 150 g (5 oz) butter. Stir well. Add to the roux.

77. Grilled Fish West Indian Style

Serves 4

600 g (generous 1 1/4 lb) fillets sea bass
Juice of 1 lemon
Salt, white pepper
1 tsp whole allspice
Fresh fennel stalks
1 clove garlic
1 tbsp chopped fresh mixed herbs *or* 1 tsp
**   dried herbs**
1 tbsp chopped fresh parsley *or* 1 tsp dried
**   parsley**
8 tbsp olive oil

Soak the fillets for several hours in a cool
place in a marinade of the lemon juice, salt,
pepper, and allspice. Arrange the fennel on a
hot grill and cook the fish on top of it for
3 minutes on each side.

Crush the garlic in a mortar with the
mixed herbs and parsley. Add enough olive
oil to form a smooth sauce. Serve the grilled
fillets on this sauce.

78. Grilled Haddock

Serves 4

800 g (1 3/4 lb) haddock fillets
Pepper
Butter, melted
Maître d'hôtel butter (Recipe 17)

Season the haddock fillets with pepper and
brush them with melted butter. Grill very
gently over the barbecue, basting frequently
with melted butter. Cook for 12 minutes,
turning 3 times. Serve with maître d'hôtel
butter.

79. Barbecued Herring

Serves 4

800 g (1 3/4 lb) fresh herring
Salt, white pepper
Oil
Mustard butter (100 g butter, 1 tbsp
**   mustard, and 1 tsp fresh tarragon *or***
**   pinch dried tarragon)**

Scale the herring and clean them through
the gill openings, without cutting into the
abdomen. With a very sharp knife make
shallow slashes in the backs of the fish.
Season with salt and pepper and dip in oil.
Grill over a very hot barbecue for 3 minutes
on each side. Serve with a mustard butter, to
which you can add the herring roe or milt.

80. Grilled Mackerel

Serves 4

4 small whole mackerel, 200 g (scant 1/2 lb)
** each**
Salt, white pepper
Oil
Saucepan water
250 g (1/2 lb) gooseberries
2 tbsp butter
1 tbsp flour
400 ml (1 3/4 cups) cold water
Nutmeg
Dash vinegar
1 tbsp fresh dill leaves *or* 1 tsp dried dill

Clean the mackerel through the gill openings, without cutting into the abdomen. Make 2 incisions across the backbone, each 2 cm (3/4″) deep. Season with salt and pepper and sprinkle well with oil. Set aside in a cool place for 30 minutes.

In the meantime boil a saucepan of water on a corner of the barbecue. Plunge the gooseberries into this water for 2 minutes. Drain, discarding the water; set the gooseberries aside to dry. In the same pan make a roux with the butter and flour. Stir in the cold water to make a white sauce and season it with salt, pepper, and nutmeg. Add the vinegar and dry gooseberries. Stir well with a wooden spoon. Add the dill, snipped with scissors or a very sharp knife.

Barbecue the mackerel for 7 minutes on each side. Arrange on a platter, bathed in the gooseberry sauce.

Note: As well as a very *nouvelle cuisine* counterpoint of flavors and textures, this recipe makes a very French play on words. In French gooseberries are "mackerel currants."

81. Red Mullet with Sea Urchin Paste

Serves 4

8 red mullet,* very fresh (the abdomens must be firm)
Olive oil
Salt, white pepper
Sprigs dried fennel
2 dozen sea urchins

Scale but do not clean the mullet; remove only the gills. Marinate in a little oil, salt, and pepper; cover and leave in a cool place for 30 minutes. Grill over coals on which you have burned dried fennel (if possible), or over plain charcoal, for 2 minutes on each side. Keep hot while you prepare the sea urchins.

Crush the orange insides of the sea urchins thoroughly in a mortar and coat the mullet with this delicious paste before serving.

*Since the days of the Romans (who wrote about the red mullet with great enthusiasm) those who know this little fish have insisted that it is incomparable, that there is no conceivable substitute for it. Unfortunately, this delicacy is found only in the Mediterranean and some nearby waters. Still, the recipes for red mullet in this cookbook are sufficiently unusual that you may want to try them with other small, tasty, white-fleshed fish; at least some of the flavors will be the same.

82. Grilled Mullet with Herbs

Serves 4

**8 red mullet,* very fresh (the abdomens
must be firm)**
4 tbsp olive oil
Salt, fresh-ground pepper
1 clove garlic, minced or well mashed
4 tbsp vinegar
120 ml (1/2 cup) dry white wine
Juice of half a lemon
1 tsp tomato paste
**Pinch fresh thyme *or* small pinch dried
thyme**
Dash anisette
Chopped fresh mint

Scale but do not clean the mullet; remove
only the gills. Rinse and dry well. Sprinkle
with oil, salt, and pepper. While the grill is
warming, place the garlic and oil in a bowl
and mix well. Add the remaining ingredients
except for the mint.

Grill the mullet for 2 minutes on each
side. (Place the fish diagonally on the grill
and give them a quarter turn after each
minute.) Arrange on a warm serving dish.
Pour the sauce over the mullet, sprinkle
with the fresh mint, and serve immediately.

Variation: You can serve grilled mullet with
anchovy butter instead of this herb sauce.
Mash 4 anchovy fillets with 80 g (3 oz)
butter. When the mixture is smooth, add a
few drops of lemon juice and 3 turns of the
pepper mill. Serve separately.

*See note to Recipe 81.

83. Grilled Sardines with Cider

Serves 4

16 fresh sardines
250 ml (1 cup) dry cider
1 apple
2 tbsp walnut oil
1 tbsp Calvados
1 tbsp prepared hot mustard
1 tbsp *crème fraîche**
Salt, white pepper

Clean the sardines. Marinate for 30 minutes in the cider. Cut an apple into small slivers and mix into the remaining ingredients. Stuff the sardines with this mixture and close them. Brush with oil. Grill for 2 minutes on each side.

  *See note to Recipe 28.

84. Barbecued Sole

Serves 4

4 sole, 300 g (generous 1/2 lb) each, cleaned and dressed when you buy them
Salt, white pepper
Oil
500 ml (2 cups) thick cream *or* 35% cream, such as whipping cream
4 tbsp chopped fresh herbs *or* 4 tsp dried herbs

Lightly score the white side of the fish with the point of a sharp knife. Season with salt and pepper. Brush with oil and place on a hot barbecue, white side down. After 4 minutes turn carefully with a spatula and grill for another 4 minutes. Meanwhile, on a corner of the barbecue heat the cream and herbs. Season with salt and pepper.

Carefully lift the top (white side) fillet from each fish and remove the bones from underneath it (this will be easier if you broke the spine in 2 or 3 places before grilling), or let your guests do this for themselves. Replace the top fillet on the now boneless fish and serve with a bowl of the herb sauce.

85. Grilled Baby Sole

Serves 4

12 baby sole *or* butterfish — another small,
  rather flat fish
Salt, white pepper
Flour
Butter, melted
Fresh parsley, shredded with scissors
Lemon wedges

Scale and clean the fish and score them
lightly across the back with a sharp knife.
Season with salt and pepper. Dip in flour,
then moisten well with melted butter.

  Grill gently over the barbecue, sprinkling
occasionally with melted butter. Cook for 5
minutes on each side. Sprinkle with the
parsley and garnish with lemon wedges.

86. Tuna Steak

Serves 4

1 large tuna steak, about 1 kg (2 1/4 lb)
Salt, white pepper
2 tbsp olive oil
2 tbsp dry white wine
Juice of 1 lemon
1 onion, minced
1 clove garlic, minced
Bouquet garni
Shallot butter (Recipe 10)
Tomato wedges

Season the tuna steak with salt and pepper.
Marinate for 1 hour in a cool place in a
mixture of the oil, wine, lemon juice, onion,
garlic, and bouquet garni. Turn frequently.

  Grill the marinated tuna for about
20 minutes, turning 3 times. Brush with the
marinade as often as possible, as tuna meat
is naturally quite dry. Serve with shallot
butter and tomato wedges.

87. Shrimp Irish Style

Serves 4

1 kg (2 1/4 lb) whole, unshelled shrimp
Fresh-ground white pepper
100 ml (1/3 cup) whisky, preferably Irish

Heat a large, heavy frying pan directly over
the coals. When the bottom of the pan is
almost red hot, toss in the shrimp. Cook for
5 minutes, shaking the pan constantly. Add
pepper.

Off the fire pour the whisky over the
shrimp. Flambé and serve immediately.

88. Grilled Shrimp *au Naturel*

Serves 4

1 kg (2 1/4 lb) whole, unshelled shrimp
White pepper
Olive oil
Lemon wedges

Heat a large, heavy frying pan directly over
the coals. When the bottom of the pan is
almost red hot, toss in the shrimp and cook
for a few minutes, shaking the pan
continuously. Add the pepper while the
shrimp are cooking.

Serve on a hot dish, with olive oil and
lemon wedges on the table.

89. Barbecued Scampi

Serves 4

2 dozen scampi (marine crayfish) *or* very
**   large shrimp tails**
Olive oil
Salt, fresh-ground white pepper
Lemon juice
2 tbsp butter
2 cloves garlic, peeled
1 tbsp chopped fresh parsley *or* 1 tsp dried
**   parsley**
Dash Tabasco sauce

Split the scampi shells along the underside
with a pair of very sharp scissors, taking
care not to cut into the flesh. Brush liberally
with oil and season with salt and pepper.
Barbecue for 2 minutes on each side,
starting with the split side down. Arrange on
a hot platter and sprinkle with lemon juice.

Place a small pot on the barbecue and
melt the butter with the garlic; add the
parsley and Tabasco sauce. Serve the grilled
scampi sprinkled with butter sauce.

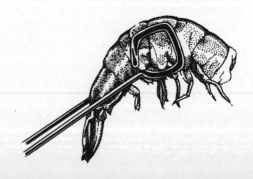

90. Grilled Lobster

Serves 4

**2 lobsters, 1.2 kg (2 1/2 lb) each
Salt, white pepper
Butter, melted
Cognac *or* sherry**

Split the lobsters in two lengthwise. Remove the intestines and the stomach. Season with salt and pepper. Place the lobster halves on a very hot grill (the coals should be white), shell side down. Grill for 10 minutes, basting the flesh from time to time with melted butter.

After 10 minutes turn and grill the meat for 2 minutes, then turn again onto the shell and cook for another 2 minutes, basting constantly with the melted butter. Serve very hot, sprinkled with a little cognac or sherry.

Variation: You can also serve lobster with mayonnaise flavored with the creamy parts inside the head.

91. Grilled Scallops

Serves 4

**16 large scallops
Salt, white pepper
Lemon juice
Fresh parsley, chopped**

On a hot, well-oiled grill cook the scallops for 30 seconds on each side. Season with salt and pepper. Moisten with lemon juice. Sprinkle with the parsley and serve immediately.

92. Grilled Escargots

Per person

**100 g (3 1/2 oz) butter
1 tbsp chopped fresh parsley *or* 1 tsp dried
   parsley
Garlic, crushed
Juice of half a lemon
Salt, white pepper
1 dozen escargots, precooked or canned**

Cream the butter in a mortar. Add the parsley, garlic, lemon juice, salt, and pepper. Work this mixture into a smooth paste. Put the escargots into their shells and seal the shells with this butter mixture. Grill for 7 minutes on an already hot grill.

POULTRY AND GAME

93. Chicken Breasts Japanese Style

Serves 4

400 ml (1 3/4 cups) soy sauce
200 ml (3/4 cup) sherry
200 ml (3/4 cup) chicken stock, canned or
** homemade**
4 chicken breasts, deboned but with the
** skin on**
1 tbsp castor sugar
1 tbsp cornstarch or arrowroot
2 tbsp prepared hot mustard
Sprigs parsley

Heat the grill well, using charcoal. Prepare a marinade with the soy sauce, sherry, and chicken stock. Bring to a boil and allow to cool. Dip in the chicken breasts. Grill for 3 minutes, skin side up. Dip in the marinade again and grill for 3 minutes, skin side down. Dip once more in the marinade and grill for 4 minutes, skin side up.

While the chicken is cooking, whisk 4 tbsp marinade with the sugar, cornstarch or arrowroot, and mustard. Cook gently on a corner of the barbecue until they form a syrup.

Cut the grilled chicken breasts into bite-sized pieces and arrange on warmed individual plates. Pour the thick mustard sauce over the top. Serve immediately, garnished with the sprigs of parsley.

94. Grilled Breast of Duck

Serves 4

2 duck breasts, deboned but with the skin
** on**
Salt, white pepper
75 ml (1/4 cup) olive oil
150 ml (2/3 cup) red wine
Herb butter

Score the skins of the duck breasts. Season with salt and pepper on both sides. Marinate in a mixture of the oil and wine in a covered dish; leave for 24 hours in a cool place.

On the day of the barbecue drain the breasts and pat dry with a paper towel. Grill skin side down for 10 minutes, then flesh side down for 3 minutes. Wrap in aluminum foil and let stand for 10 minutes. This allows the juices concentrated in the center to spread all through the meat, giving it a pleasing smoothness. Serve on a hot platter with the herb butter.

Variation: Substitute a piece of chuck beef for the duck breasts and grill it to taste — rare, medium rare, etc. Allow 220 g (7 oz) meat per person.

95. Escalopes of Goose with Lemon

Serves 4

Juice of 5 lemons
200 ml (3/4 cup) sherry
2 sprigs fresh basil *or* 2 tbsp dried basil
Pinch ground allspice
800 g (1 3/4 lb) goose breast, deboned, skinned, and cut into thin, lengthwise slices (if goose is not available, substitute whole, skinned, and deboned duck breasts, split into 2 flat slices)
150 g (5 oz) butter, softened
Salt, white pepper

Make a marinade with the juice of 4 lemons, the sherry, basil, and allspice. Marinate the meat for 4 hours in a cool place, turning occasionally. Meanwhile, cream the butter with the remaining lemon juice and the salt and pepper.

Pat the meat dry, then coat with the lemon butter, keeping back about 1 tablespoonful. Grill over a hot barbecue for 8 minutes (less if you are grilling duck),

turning every 2 minutes. Take care not to pierce the meat. Season with salt after about 4 minutes. When cooked, cut as necessary and serve on warmed plates.

96. Grilled Pigeons in Breadcrumbs

Serves 4

4 young pigeons (squab)
Lemon juice
Butter, melted
Salt, white pepper
Stale breadcrumbs
Sauce Diable (Recipe 39)

Tie each pigeon's feet together, then split the birds down the back, following the spine, and spread them flat. Flatten with a mallet and sprinkle with lemon juice. Press between 2 plates and set aside for 2 hours in a cool place with a weight on each pair of plates.

Season the butter with salt and pepper. Brush the pigeons with this mixture and dip them in breadcrumbs. Grill very gently for 20 minutes over white coals, sprinkling with melted butter from time to time. Turn and repeat for 20 minutes on the other side. Serve with Sauce Diable.

97. Grilled Partridge

Serves 4

2 large, young partridge *or* grouse
Salt, white pepper
Olive oil
4 large mushroom caps
100 g (3 1/2 oz) butter, softened
1 tbsp finely chopped fresh parsley *or* 1 tsp dried parsley
2 cloves garlic, crushed
Lemon juice

Split the partridges along the back, flatten them, and with a very sharp, pointed knife remove the small bones from the front of the breast. Season with salt and pepper, then marinate in a little oil for 1 hour in a covered dish in a cool place.

Grill for 5 minutes on each side on a hot, oiled grill, basting from time to time with a little marinade. Set aside and keep warm on a serving dish. Dip the mushroom caps in the marinade and grill for 5 minutes on each side. While they are cooking, prepare the parsley butter by working the parsley and garlic thoroughly into the butter.

Place the grilled mushroom caps on the serving dish with the partridges. Sprinkle with lemon juice. Serve with the parsley butter in a separate dish.

98. Grilled Saddle of Young Rabbit

Serves 4

4 tbsp olive oil
Juice of 1 lemon
2 cloves garlic, crushed
1 tsp fresh savory *or* pinch dried savory
1 small hot red pepper, very finely chopped
Saddle* of 2 young rabbits, cut into 8 pieces
White pepper
8 slices bacon
Salt

To prepare the marinade, mix the oil, lemon juice, garlic, savory, and chopped pepper. Marinate the rabbit for 2 hours in a cool place, turning from time to time.

Pat the meat dry, season with pepper, and wrap each piece in a slice of bacon. Secure with a wooden toothpick. Grill gently for no longer than 30 minutes, turning frequently and basting with the marinade. Remove from the heat. Salt lightly before serving.

*In French, *râble*: the entire back from leg to shoulder, well trimmed.

PORK

99. Grilled Pork with Mustard

Serves 4

4 large, thin slices lean pork, 200 g (scant 1/2 lb) each
Salt, black pepper
Oil
100 g (3 1/2 oz) sweet butter, softened
3 tsp prepared hot mustard
1 tsp chopped fresh tarragon *or* pinch dried tarragon
1 tsp lemon juice
Lemon wedges

Season the pork with salt and pepper. Brush with oil. Blend the butter, mustard, tarragon, and lemon juice until smooth.

Grill the pork gently for 4 minutes. Turn. Spread one-third of the mustard butter on the cooked side of the meat and cook for 4 minutes longer. Turn and repeat, using the second third of the mustard butter. Cook for 4 minutes. Turn again and grill for 4 minutes more. Arrange on a hot serving dish and spread with the remaining mustard butter. Garnish with lemon wedges.

100. Pork Tenderloin Creole

Serves 4

8 pieces pork tenderloin, about 100 g (3 1/2 oz) each
Coarse salt
Oil
16 thin slices bacon
4 slices fresh pineapple, each cut into 4 pieces
Black pepper
Lime wedges

Sprinkle the meat with coarse salt and set aside in a cool place for 2 hours, then dry thoroughly and brush with oil. Wrap a slice of bacon around each piece of fresh pineapple. Secure with a wooden toothpick.

Grill everything on the barbecue for 10 minutes or so, turning frequently. Season with pepper before serving. Garnish with lime wedges.

101. Grilled Medallions of Pork

Serves 4

12 thick slices pork tenderloin
2 tbsp olive oil
Juice of 1 lemon
1 tsp powdered cumin
1 tbsp chopped fresh rosemary *or* 1 tsp
  dried rosemary
Salt, white pepper
Butter, melted

Use a mallet to flatten the medallions
slightly. Marinate in a cool place for 2 hours
in a mixture of the oil, lemon juice, cumin,
rosemary, salt, and pepper. Stir from time to
time.

  Preheat the grill. Dry the medallions well,
place on the grill, and cook for about 10
minutes, turning frequently. Sprinkle with a
few drops of melted butter before serving.

102. Grilled Pork Chops

Serves 4

4 pork loin chops, 200 g (scant 1/2 lb) each
50 ml (scant 1/4 cup) cognac
250 ml (1 cup) dry white wine
1 tbsp lemon juice
4 tbsp olive oil
2 carrots, thinly sliced
2 shallots, thinly sliced
1 stick celery, thinly sliced
Bouquet garni
4 pinches salt
Black pepper (8 turns of the pepper mill)
Prepared hot mustard

Marinate the chops in the cognac, wine,
lemon juice, oil, vegetables, bouquet garni,
salt, and pepper in a cool place for 2 hours.

  Pat the excess marinade from the chops,
then spread them with mustard. Grill for
15 minutes. Turn often and baste from time
to time with the bouquet garni soaked in
marinade. Serve with a green salad with
walnuts and thinly sliced apples.

103. Pork Chops with Paprika

Serves 4

4 pork rib chops, about 250 g (1/2 lb) each
Coarse salt
3 green bell peppers
50 g (1 3/4 oz) paprika
Pinch salt
2 pinches white pepper
120 ml (1/2 cup) red wine
Olive oil

Sprinkle the pork with coarse salt and set aside in a cool place for 2 hours.

Seed the peppers and put them through a blender. In a small serving bowl mix the paprika, salt, pepper, and wine. Add the pepper puree. Refrigerate.

Dry the pork chops and brush with oil. Grill for about 20 minutes. Serve very hot with the well-chilled paprika sauce.

104. Pork Chops with Lime and Sage

Serves 4

4 pork chops, about 250 g (1/2 lb) each
Juice of 4 limes
4 tbsp olive oil
50 g (2 oz) fresh sage leaves *or* 1 tsp dried
**   sage**
4 leaves fresh mint *or* 1/2 tsp dried mint
Salt, black pepper

Marinate the pork chops in the lime juice, oil, sage, and mint in a cool place for 2 hours. Pat dry. Grill for 5 minutes on each side, sprinkling from time to time with the marinade. Season with salt halfway through cooking. Sprinkle generously with pepper before serving.

105. Pig's Feet Sainte-Ménehould

Serves 4

4 pig's feet, precooked and split
Butter, melted
Breadcrumbs
150 ml (2/3 cup) dry white wine
1 tbsp lemon juice
1 tbsp prepared hot mustard
Salt, fresh-ground pepper
50 g (1 3/4 oz) cold, fresh butter
2 tbsp chopped fresh parsley *or* 2 tsp dried parsley

Dip the pig's feet in melted butter, then roll in breadcrumbs. Grill for 15 minutes, turning frequently and sprinkling with melted butter from time to time.

While the meat is cooking, place a mixture of the wine, lemon juice, and mustard in a small pan on a corner of the barbecue and reduce to half. Remove from the heat and season with salt and pepper. Add the cold butter a little at a time, beating in with a small whisk. Add the parsley.

Serve the pig's feet with the mustard sauce in a separate dish.

106. Grilled Pork Ribs

Serves 4

4 tbsp peanut oil
2 onions, chopped
4 tbsp soy sauce
2 tbsp sherry
2 tsp castor sugar
1.5 kg (scant 3 1/4 lb) extra-meaty spare ribs, cut into serving pieces

On a corner of the barbecue in a small pot heat the oil and cook the onions until golden. Add the soy sauce, sherry, and sugar. Cook for 5 minutes more, stirring with a wooden spoon. Allow to cool.

Place the pork ribs in a large bowl and coat thoroughly with the cooled marinade. Set aside in a cool place for approximately 4 hours; stir from time to time.

Light the barbecue. When the coals are white, heat the grill, which should be at least 8 inches away from the coals. Grill the ribs for 40 minutes, turning often. They should be well browned. Serve immediately with potatoes baked in foil for 30 minutes in the barbecue coals and with a herb-flavored white cheese.

VEAL

107. Grilled Escalopes of Veal

Serves 4

Juice of 2 lemons
Salt, fresh-ground white pepper
2 sprigs fresh rosemary *or* 1 tbsp dried rosemary
1 onion, very finely chopped
1 clove garlic, crushed
4 tbsp olive oil
8 veal cutlets, about 100 g (scant 1/4 lb) each
Butter, melted
Breadcrumbs

Prepare a marinade with the lemon juice, salt, pepper, rosemary, onion, garlic, and oil. Marinate the cutlets for 1 hour in a cool place.

Drain the meat and pat dry. Brush with melted butter and roll in breadcrumbs. Grill gently for 10 minutes on each side, sprinkling from time to time with melted butter seasoned with lemon juice. Season with salt when half cooked. Season with pepper just before serving.

108. Veal Chops with Sage

Serves 4

Juice of 1 lemon
4 tbsp lard, melted
30 leaves fresh sage, chopped, *or* 3 tbsp dried sage
3 leaves fresh mint, chopped, *or* 1 tsp dried mint
Fresh-ground white pepper
4 veal rib chops, about 250 g (1/2 lb) each, with "tail" meat removed so that the last 5 cm (2″) or so of rib bone is bare
Salt

Prepare a thick marinade by mixing the lemon juice, lard, sage, mint, and pepper. Coat the veal chops with this mixture and leave in a cool place for 1 hour.

Grill the chops gently on the barbecue for 10 minutes on each side. Salt them when half cooked. Season with pepper just before serving.

109. Veal Rolls Italian Style

Serves 4

8 thin veal cutlets
Salt, fresh-ground white pepper
100 g (3 1/2 oz) breadcrumbs
5 tbsp milk, warmed
100 g (3 1/2 oz) semisoft goat's milk
** cheese, crushed**
1 tbsp chopped fresh parsley *or* 1 tsp dried
** parsley**
1 clove garlic, minced
4 tbsp olive oil

Flatten the cutlets with the blade of a large kitchen knife. Season with salt and pepper. Stir the breadcrumbs into the milk to make a paste, then add the cheese and parsley. Mix well. Add the garlic, salt, and pepper.

Divide this mixture among the cutlets and roll each up around its filling. Secure with a wooden toothpick. Oil the rolls and place on a very hot grill. Cook for about 15 minutes, turning frequently. Serve immediately.

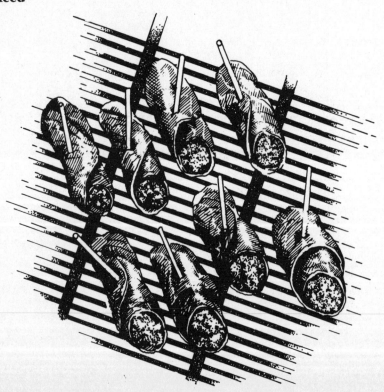

BEEF

110. Beef Tenderloin with Herbes de Provence

Serves 4

Juice of 1 lemon
100 ml (about 1/3 cup) olive oil
Fresh-ground white pepper
50 g (1 3/4 oz) fresh thyme flowers *or* 2 tsp dried thyme
50 g (1 3/4 oz) fresh rosemary leaves *or* 2 tsp dried rosemary
2 bay leaves
50 g (1 3/4 oz) chopped fresh basil *or* 2 tsp dried basil
1 clove garlic, crushed
4 slices beef tenderloin, about 200 g (scant 1/2 lb) each
Salt
Aïoli (Recipe 21)

Prepare the marinade in an earthenware pot by mixing together the lemon juice, oil, pepper, herbs, and garlic. Marinate the beef for 2 hours in a cool place.

Grill the beef for 3 minutes on each side. Season with pepper and salt just before serving. Serve with a bowl of aïoli.

111. Tournedos on Slate

Serves 6

6 beef tournedos (center-cut tenderloin steaks)
Salt, white pepper

Heat 6 pieces of slate, approximately the size of large dinner plates, in the coals of the barbecue. When they are very hot, remove them from the fire, quickly rinse off any ashes, and place 1 steak on each.

The heat remaining in the slates will cook the meat very quickly. Turn after 2 minutes and season the cooked side of the meat with salt and pepper. Start to eat while it is still cooking. The slate gives the meat a unique flavor and keeps it hot right up to the last mouthful.

112. Contre-Filet Périgord* Style

Serves 4

2 thick club, striploin, *or* New York cut**
steaks, about 500 g (generous 1 lb) when
well trimmed
Oil
Fresh-ground white pepper
Salt
1 large truffle, cut into thick slices
Butter

Prepare the barbecue. When the grill is very hot, brush the steaks lightly with oil and pepper well. Grill for 2 minutes, turn 90°, and grill 2 minutes longer. This will sear them in a grid pattern, forming a protective crust on the surface of the meat. Season with salt and arrange the slices of truffle and little knobs of butter on each steak.

When the butter melts, remove the truffle slices and turn the steak. Arrange the truffle slices on the cooked side, with more little knobs of butter, repeating the searing process. When the butter has melted on the second side, the steaks are ready. Serve very hot.

*See note to Recipe 68.
**These are regional names for the same cut, which is relatively new to this continent. Your butcher should know at least one of them.

113. Chilean Entrecôtes

Serves 4

4 onions, minced
1 clove garlic, minced or well mashed
1 tbsp fresh parsley, shredded with
scissors, *or* 1 tsp dried parsley
3 tbsp vinegar
Juice of 1 lemon
Pinch cayenne pepper
Salt
2 boneless rib steaks, about 500 g
(generous 1 lb) each, trimmed
Oil
Fresh-ground white pepper

Heat the grill. To prepare the Chilean sauce, mix together in a bowl the onions, garlic, parsley, vinegar, lemon juice, cayenne, and salt. Set aside.

Brush the steaks with oil and season with salt and pepper. Place on the hot grill and cook for 10 minutes on each side. Cut each steak in two, arrange on a hot platter, and cover with the Chilean sauce. Serve immediately.

114. Entrecôtes Tuscan Style

Serves 4

**2 boneless rib steaks, about 500 g
(generous 1 lb) each, trimmed
Fresh-ground black pepper
Olive oil
Lemon wedges
Salt**

Fifteen minutes before the steaks are to be cooked, season them generously with pepper and brush with oil. Grill for 4 minutes on each side. Season with salt and sprinkle with a few drops of oil just before serving. Garnish with lemon wedges.

115. Rib of Beef with Anchoïade

Serves 4

**200 g (7 oz) anchovy fillets, rinsed well to
remove the salt, *or* 2 small cans flat
anchovy fillets, drained
4 cloves garlic
4 sprigs fresh tarragon *or* 4 tbsp dried
tarragon
Fresh-ground black pepper
50 ml (scant 1/4 cup) olive oil
Juice of 1 lemon
1 very thick rib steak, about 1.5 kg (scant
3 1/4 lb)
Salt**

To prepare the anchoïade, puree the anchovy fillets, garlic, and tarragon in a mortar. Season with pepper and work in, a little at a time, the oil, then the lemon juice. You should obtain a thick sauce.

Salt the meat very lightly and brush with oil. Grill for 5 minutes; turn a quarter turn and grill 5 minutes longer. Turn, salt lightly, and repeat on the other side. Season with pepper. Allow to stand for 10 minutes in a warm place before carving. Spread the anchoïade over the bottom of a hot platter and serve the sliced beef on top.

116. Rib of Beef Niçoise

Serves 4

**1 very thick rib steak, about 1.5 kg (scant
    3 1/4 lb)**
Olive oil
Salt, white pepper
4 tomatoes, peeled, seeded, and crushed
1 clove garlic, minced or finely mashed
1 tsp anchovy paste
1 tbsp capers
12 black olives
**1 tbsp fresh tarragon, shredded with
    scissors, *or* 1 tsp dried tarragon**

The grill should be very hot. Brush the meat
with oil. Season with salt and pepper. Place
on the hot grill and roast for 15 minutes on
each side. Take care not to pierce the meat
when you turn it.

Meanwhile, on a corner of the barbecue
prepare the tomato sauce niçoise. Heat
2 tbsp olive oil in a pan, add the tomato
pulp, and cook for about 20 minutes. Add
the garlic, anchovy paste, capers, and olives
and season with pepper. Cook 5 minutes
longer. Remove from the fire and add the
tarragon.

Carve the meat onto a hot platter. Pour
the carving juices into the tomato sauce and
serve it over the meat.

117. Grilled Sirloin Tip with Chipolatas

Serves 4

**8 tbsp Japanese teriyaki sauce (from
    specialty grocery stores)**
2 tbsp prepared hot mustard
3 tbsp peanut oil
Few drops Tabasco sauce
Fresh-ground white pepper
4 slices sirloin tip, 200 g (scant 1/2 lb) each
8 chipolata (cocktail) sausages
Salt

Prepare a thick marinade by mixing
together the teriyaki sauce, mustard, oil,
Tabasco sauce, and pepper. Coat the steaks
and chipolatas with marinade and set aside
in a cool place for 1 hour.

Drain the steaks and grill for 3 minutes on
each side, basting with the marinade. Prick
the chipolatas with a fork and grill them at
the same time. Serve the steaks surrounded
by chipolatas. Salt to taste.

If you wish to serve a completely North
American meal, serve this with corn on the
cob!

118. Grilled Sirloin with Roquefort Butter

Serves 4

Thin-cut sirloin steak, 800 g (1 3/4 lb) after boning and trimming, cut into 4 serving pieces
Fresh-ground white pepper
Peanut oil
100 g (3 1/2 oz) butter, softened
100 g (3 1/2 oz) Roquefort cheese
20 ml (3/4 oz) cognac
1 tsp lemon juice
Salt

Pepper the sirloin steaks generously and brush with oil. Set aside for 15 minutes. Meanwhile, work the butter, Roquefort, cognac, and lemon juice into a smooth paste.

Grill the steaks for no more than 2 minutes on each side. Season lightly with salt as they finish cooking. Arrange on a hot platter and spread with Roquefort butter. Serve immediately.

119. Butcher's Tenderloin with Shallots

Serves 4

4 thick slices butcher's tenderloin,* 200 g (scant 1/2 lb) each
Fresh-ground white pepper
Oil
Salt
8 shallots, very finely chopped
100 g (3 1/2 oz) butter

Season the steaks with pepper and brush with oil 30 minutes before cooking. Grill quickly over a hot fire for no more than 2 minutes on each side. Season with salt and pepper. Arrange on a heated serving plate and cover with the shallots. Sprinkle with small knobs of butter.

Butcher's tenderloin (the bit the butcher is reputed to take home!) is believed by some connoisseurs to be the best part of the whole steer; no other piece is quite so rich in flavor. On this continent, however, it is usually ground into hamburger. Still, you may be lucky enough to find it: it may be called *back steak*, *gravy steak*, or even *boot steak* (from the delivery person's rubber boot that often hides it).

120. Peking Grill

Serves 4

2 tbsp Chinese shao-shing wine *or* sherry
2 tbsp soy sauce
1 tbsp cornstarch
1 clove garlic, crushed
6 tbsp peanut oil
**8 center-cut tenderloin steaks, 100 g (scant
    1/4 lb) each**
Fresh-ground white pepper, salt
**12 green onions, cut into 7.5-cm (3″)
    lengths and with roots removed**

Prepare the marinade in an earthenware
bowl, mixing together the wine or sherry,
soy sauce, cornstarch, garlic, and oil.
Marinate the steaks in a cool place for
2 hours.

Barbecue the steaks for 3 minutes on
each side. Season generously with pepper
and sparingly with salt just before serving.
Serve with the green onion.

121. Hamburgers with Mint

Serves 4

800 g (1 3/4 lb) ground beef
**50 g (1 3/4 oz) chopped fresh mint *or*
    12 g (1/2 oz) dried mint**
2 cloves garlic, minced
1 onion, very finely chopped
Salt, fresh-ground white pepper
Peanut oil

Knead the ground beef, mint, garlic, onion,
salt, and pepper together thoroughly.
Divide this mixture into 8 equal parts and
form into flat patties. Brush with oil. Grill
for 2 or 3 minutes on each side.

122. Grilled Beef Rolls

Serves 4

3 tbsp sherry
250 ml (1 cup) soy sauce
3 tbsp poultry stock
**4 very thin, oblong slices lean beef (sirloin
    or top round), about 150 g (over 1/4 lb)
    each**
Salt, white pepper
4 young leeks, split in two lengthwise

Prepare a marinade with the sherry, soy
sauce, and stock. Boil, then allow to cool.

Flatten the slices of meat with a mallet and
season with salt and pepper. Arrange 2 leek
halves on each piece, roll the meat up
around them, and secure with wooden
toothpicks. Dip the rolls in the marinade,
then grill 1 side over the coals for 3 minutes.
Dip again in marinade and grill for 3 minutes
on the other side. Serve immediately.

LAMB

123. Moorish Lamb Cutlets

Serves 4

20 ml (3/4 oz) olive oil
Juice of 1 lemon
1 tsp saffron
1 tsp cinnamon
Salt, fresh-ground white pepper
1 clove garlic, crushed
8 thick lamb rib chops, deboned
Harissa sauce (note to Recipe 6)
Lemon wedges

In a large salad bowl prepare the marinade by mixing the oil, lemon juice, saffron, cinnamon, salt, pepper, and garlic.

Add the lamb. Make sure it is well coated with marinade. Refrigerate for 2 hours, then grill for 3 minutes on each side. Serve with harissa sauce and garnish with lemon wedges.

124. Lamb Chops à la Provençale

Serves 4

1 tbsp thyme flowers *or* 1 tsp dried thyme
100 ml (1/3 cup) olive oil
4 very small eggplants
Coarse salt
1 clove garlic, chopped
Parsley, chopped
8 thick lamb rib chops
4 tomatoes
Salt, white pepper

Heat a cast-iron grill. Soak the thyme flowers in the oil. Cut the eggplants into thick rounds and peel. Sprinkle with coarse salt and set aside for 20 minutes. Wipe dry, sprinkle with the thyme-scented oil, and grill for 5 minutes on each side. Sprinkle with a mixture of garlic and parsley and keep hot on a platter.

Brush the lamb chops with the thyme-scented oil and grill for 3 minutes on each side. Cut the tomatoes horizontally in two, sprinkle with the thyme oil, and cook at the same time as the chops. Season with salt and pepper and sprinkle with parsley. Serve the grilled chops at once, very hot, garnished with the tomatoes and eggplants.

125. Noisettes of Lamb with Garlic Puree

Serves 4

8 cloves garlic, blanched for 2 minutes
Salt, fresh-ground white pepper
8 noisettes* of lamb
Olive oil

Mash the garlic in a mortar with a pinch of
salt. Coat the noisettes of lamb with this
garlic puree, then brush carefully with olive
oil. Grill for 3 minutes on each side. Season
with salt and pepper just before serving.

*The round ''nut'' of lean meat removed
from rib chops. The chops should be cut to
the same thickness as the diameter of the
noisette — about 5 cm (2″).

126. Leg Steaks of Mutton with Mint

Serves 4

4 center slices from a leg of mutton
50 g (1 3/4 oz) fresh mint leaves *or* 12 g
 (1/2 oz) dried mint
Fresh-ground white pepper
4 tbsp olive oil
Juice of 3 lemons
Salt

Arrange the slices of mutton side by side on
a platter. Scatter the mint leaves over them
and sprinkle with the pepper, oil, and juice
of 2 lemons. Let the meat stand for 4 hours
in a cool place.

Grill for 3 minutes on each side. Season
with salt, pepper, and the remaining lemon
juice just before serving.

127. Grilled Lamb Patties

Serves 4

Handful breadcrumbs
Milk
800 g (1 3/4 lb) lean ground lamb
1 clove garlic, minced or finely mashed
2 shallots, finely chopped
1 tsp powdered cumin
Salt, fresh-ground white pepper
1 pork caul,* cut into 4 pieces
Tabasco sauce

Soak the breadcrumbs in milk, then squeeze
them dry. Mix the ground lamb, drained
breadcrumbs, garlic, shallots, cumin, salt,
and pepper in a bowl and knead together
well.

Shape the mixture into 4 patties and wrap
each in a piece of caul. Grill for 3 minutes on
each side. Sprinkle with a few drops of
Tabasco sauce just before serving.

*A fatty membrane used to wrap certain
 prepared meats. Unless you have a
 European butcher, you may have to obtain
 your caul from a slaughterhouse. A
 possible substitute is very thin sheets of
 pork fat, secured with string; in this case,
 roll the meat in breadcrumbs before
 grilling.

ORGAN MEAT

128. Calf's Liver with Shallot Butter

Serves 4

5 tbsp shallots, pureed
5 tbsp butter, softened
Pinch salt
Juice of half a lemon
Fresh-ground black pepper
4 tbsp olive oil
1 tsp each finely chopped fresh sage, thyme, and basil *or* 1 pinch each of these herbs, dried
4 slices calf's liver, 1 cm (less than 1/2″) thick

Prepare the shallot butter by beating together the shallot puree, butter, and salt. Refrigerate.

Prepare a marinade in a large bowl by mixing the lemon juice, pepper, oil, and herbs. Marinate the liver for 1 hour in a cool place.

Drain the liver and grill for no longer than 1 minute on each side. Take care not to pierce the meat when turning it. Serve with a knob of shallot butter on each slice.

129. Veal Kidneys with Armagnac

Serves 4

2 tbsp prepared hot mustard
50 ml (scant 1/4 cup) Armagnac
Salt, fresh-ground white pepper
4 tbsp butter, softened
4 veal kidneys, with a thin layer of fat still covering them

Work the mustard, Armagnac, salt, and pepper into the butter to make a smooth paste.

Split the kidneys in half lengthwise and place them fat side down on the barbecue. Spread the other side of the kidneys with Armagnac butter. Grill gently for about 10 minutes without turning.

130. Grilled Tripe Dijon Style

Serves 4

**Juice of 1 lemon
Salt, fresh-ground white pepper
75 ml (scant 1/3 cup) peanut oil
4 tbsp fresh parsley, shredded with
   scissors, *or* 4 tsp dried parsley
800 g (1 3/4 lb) blanched best tripe
Dijon mustard
Breadcrumbs**

To prepare the marinade, mix together the lemon juice, salt, pepper, oil, and parsley in a salad bowl.

Cut the tripe into pieces 6 cm (about 2 1/2″) square. Marinate for 1 hour in a cool place. Drain, coat with mustard, and dip in breadcrumbs. Barbecue for 5 minutes on each side. Season with pepper before serving.

131. Grilled Lamb's Liver with Parsley

Serves 4

**600 g (generous 1 1/4 lb) lamb's liver, cut
   into 1-cm (scant 1/2″) slices
Salt, fresh-ground white pepper
Peanut oil
4 tbsp chopped parsley
2 cloves garlic, chopped
Breadcrumbs
Lemon wedges**

Season the sliced liver with salt and pepper. Brush with oil and sprinkle with a mixture of the parsley and garlic. Coat with breadcrumbs. Grill for 3 minutes on each side. Serve garnished with lemon wedges.

MIXED GRILLS

132. Hungarian Mixed Grill

Allow about 70 g (2 1/2 oz) per person of each kind of meat.

Steak
Veal cutlets
Calf's liver, sliced
Very small pork rib chops
Bacon rashers
Oil
Salt, white pepper
Paprika

Place all the meats together in a salad bowl. Sprinkle with a mixture of oil, salt, pepper, and paprika. Make sure the meat is well coated with the seasonings.

Begin by grilling the pork and bacon (which need the longest cooking time); then add the veal, beef, and liver in this order. Serve on a big farm-style platter surrounded by a selection of salads: very finely shredded cabbage, sliced tomatoes, diced beets, pieces of cucumber. In a separate dish serve red and green pickled peppers.

133. Mixed Grill Supreme

Allow about 80 g (3 oz) per person of each kind of meat.

Beef tenderloin
Veal kidneys
Pork ribs (extra-meaty chunks of spare ribs)
Lamb rib chops
Oil
Salt, white pepper
Fresh parsley, chervil, thyme, and tarragon
Butter

Brush the meat with oil and add to the grill in this order: pork ribs, veal kidneys, lamb, and beef. Season with salt and pepper, sprinkle with the fresh herbs, and top with a bit of butter.

This dish combines the choicest morsels from each animal to make a supreme mixed grill.

VEGETABLES

134. Grilled Artichokes

Serves 4

**12 small, tender purple or green
   artichokes**
Salt, white pepper
Olive oil
Herb vinaigrette

Cut the artichokes in two lengthwise.
Season with salt and pepper. Dip in oil until
they are well soaked. Drain the surplus oil
from the artichokes and grill gently for
30 minutes, turning once. Serve with a bowl
of herb vinaigrette.

135. Barbecued Eggplant

Serves 4

2 small eggplants
Coarse salt
Tabasco sauce
Olive oil
Lime juice
Fresh parsley, chopped

Cut the eggplants in two lengthwise.
Sprinkle with coarse salt and set aside for
1 hour.
   Wipe the eggplant halves dry and grill for
15 minutes, turning once. Spice with a little
Tabasco sauce. Serve with a seasoning of
olive oil, lime juice, and parsley.

136. Grilled Mushrooms

Serves 4

8 large, firm *cèpes (boletus mushrooms)
  or 16 large commercial mushrooms
Walnut oil
Salt, white pepper
100 g (3 1/2 oz) butter, softened
1 tbsp finely chopped fresh parsley *or* 1 tsp
  dried parsley
2 cloves garlic, crushed**

Clean and wipe the mushrooms (do not wash them) and discard the stems. Brush with oil. Place on the barbecue and grill gently for 10 minutes on each side. Season with salt and pepper.

  While the mushrooms are cooking, prepare the parsley butter by working the parsley and garlic thoroughly into the butter. Arrange the grilled mushrooms on a dish and serve with a knob of parsley butter on each.

  *Large wild mushrooms, usually brightly colored. They are occasionally available in stores (usually dried), or you can learn to recognize them and gather them yourself.

137. Vegetable Mixed Grill

Serves 4

**4 small, very fresh zucchini
Salt
400 g (14 oz) summer squash
2 large red onions
4 heads red chicory*
1 green bell pepper
1 red bell pepper
Olive oil
White pepper**

Wipe the zucchini and cut in two lengthwise. Do not peel. Sprinkle with salt and let drain for 30 minutes. Cut the squash into large pieces. Cut the onions in two crosswise. Wash the chicory and cut off the heads at the level of the leaves. Split the peppers in two, remove the seeds, and flatten them.

  Brush all the vegetables with oil. Grill over a hot fire for 5 minutes, season with salt and pepper, turn, and grill for a further 5 minutes.

  *If not available, replace with eggplant or endive.

138. Grilled New Potatoes

Serves 4

4 large new potatoes
Salt, white pepper
Olive oil

Wash and dry the potatoes. Do not peel them. Cut lengthwise into 1-cm (scant 1/2") slices. Season with salt and pepper and brush with oil. Grill for 5 minutes on each side, turning 4 times as you would a steak, so that the bars of the grill make a grid pattern on the surface.

139. Grilled Tomatoes

Serves 4

4 large tomatoes, almost green and rather
flat
Salt, white pepper
Olive oil
Fresh rosemary leaves, very finely
chopped

Stem the tomatoes with the point of a knife, leaving a cone-shaped hole in the tops. Season with salt and pepper, brush with oil, and grill gently for 3 minutes on each side. Sprinkle with a pinch of rosemary before serving.

CHEESE

140. Barbecued Cheeses

Serves 6

1 Camembert, not too ripe
**6 dry chabichous (goat's milk cheese from
    the Poitou region of France)**
**Oil scented with herbes de Provence
    (thyme, rosemary, bay, basil; see also
    Recipe 110)**
Fresh-ground black pepper
Whole wheat bread

Scrape the outsides of the cheeses, being
sure to leave a little of the rind on them.
Brush with the oil and grill for 3 minutes on
each side. Serve with pepper and slices of
toasted whole wheat bread.

141. Cheese Mixed Grill

Serves 4

**Mixture of firm cheeses (gruyère,
    emmenthal, comté, beaufort, cheddar,
    etc.); allow 150 g (5 oz) per person**
Whole wheat bread
**Selection of fresh herbs and spices:
    parsley, basil, black pepper, caraway,
    etc.**

Cut the cheeses into slices about 1 cm (scant
1/2") thick. Grill over a hot fire for
2 minutes on each side. They should not
run. Serve immediately on a hot dish with
toasted whole wheat bread and herbs and
spices.

142. Raclette

Serves 8

Half a medium-hard raclette cheese, about 2.5 kg (5 1/2 lb)
Tart mixed pickles
Potatoes boiled in their skins
Paprika
Fresh-ground black pepper

If your barbecue is a simple firebox, stand it on end so that you have a small, concentrated bed of coals with a heat reflector above them.

Scrape the rind off the cheese. Put the cheese on a small board in front of the barbecue with the cut side facing the fire.

Wait 2 minutes until the cheese has melted, then scrape it onto a hot plate.

Your guests can season their own raclette and choose among the garnishes, washing it all down with a fruity white wine — for example, *Fendant*, the wine of the Valais region of Switzerland, where raclette originated.

FRUIT

143. Grilled Bananas

Per person

1 banana, not too ripe
1 tsp dark brown sugar
Light rum

Remove the skin from 1 side of the banana. Place the banana skin side down on the grill. Cook for 5 minutes, sprinkle with sugar, and cook for 5 more minutes. Sprinkle with rum as you serve it.

144. Grilled Apples

Per person

1 choice eating apple
Lemon juice
Sugar
Sweet butter
Cinnamon

Peel the apples and cut into horizontal slices about 2 cm (3/4″) thick and sprinkle with lemon juice so they don't turn brown. Sprinkle with sugar. Cook on a piece of buttered aluminum foil for 3 minutes on each side. Dust with a pinch of cinnamon just before serving.

VII

BROCHETTES

FISH AND SEAFOOD

145. Salmon Brochettes

Serves 4

600 g (generous 1 1/4 lb) fresh salmon
200 g (7 oz) mushrooms, halved
4 small tomatoes
4 small pieces pork fat
Butter, melted
Breadcrumbs
Salt, white pepper
Parsley, chopped
Lemon juice

Cut the salmon into 3-cm (1 1/4″) cubes.
Thread onto a skewer, alternating with
mushroom halves. Place a tomato at the tip
of each skewer and keep it in place by
adding a little chunk of pork fat. Brush the
brochettes with melted butter and dust with
breadcrumbs.

Grill for 2 minutes on each side. Season
with salt and pepper. Serve immediately,
sprinkled lightly with chopped parsley and
lemon juice.

146. Conger Eel Spanish Style

Serves 4

600 g (generous 1 1/4 lb) conger eel, cut
    into 4-cm (1 1/2″) cubes
4 tbsp olive oil
1 tsp saffron
Bay leaves
Fresh-ground pepper
200 g (7 oz) chorizo sausage,* thinly sliced
Salt

In a deep bowl soak the pieces of eel in a
marinade of the oil, saffron, 1 crumbled bay
leaf, and pepper. Leave in a cool place for 3
hours, turning occasionally.

Thread onto a skewer, alternating a piece
of eel, a slice of chorizo, and a quarter of a
bay leaf. Arrange the brochettes over the
coals and grill for 5 minutes on each side.
Season very lightly with salt before serving.

*Red sausage, a Spanish specialty. Made of
  pork flavored with red pepper and put into
  a small-sized casing.

147. Marinated Lotte Brochettes

Serves 4

600 g (generous 1 1/4 lb) lotte* *or* catfish
200 g (7 oz) streaky bacon
75 ml (scant 1/3 cup) olive oil
300 ml (1 1/3 cup) red wine
30 ml (1 oz) Armagnac
2 shallots, chopped
Salt, cayenne pepper
Thyme
Bay leaf
12 small mushroom caps
Celery, coarsely chopped
White pepper
Butter, melted
Breadcrumbs
Fresh parsley, shredded with scissors

Cut the fish into 3-cm (1 1/4″) cubes. Cut the bacon into 3-cm (1 1/4″) pieces. Prepare a marinade with the oil, wine, Armagnac, shallots, salt, cayenne, thyme, and bay leaf. Marinate the fish for 2 hours in a cool place.

Thread onto 4 skewers, alternating mushrooms, fish, bacon, and celery, ending with a mushroom. Season with salt and pepper. Brush the brochettes with melted butter and dip in breadcrumbs. Grill over white coals for 8 minutes, turning often. Sprinkle with parsley before serving.

*Angler fish. It's not often available in North America, and when it is, it's usually called *sea squab* or something similar. It's always sold dressed — it's too ugly whole to look edible. Catfish (or any bullhead) is a good substitute.

148. Sole Brochettes

Serves 4

Juice of 1 lemon
Tabasco sauce
Salt, white pepper
4 tbsp olive oil
Half a bulb fresh fennel, very thinly sliced,
  ***or* 2 tsp dried fennel**
600 g (generous 1 1/4 lb) fillets of sole
4 tomatoes, quartered
100 g (3 1/2 oz) bacon, thinly sliced
Butter, melted
Breadcrumbs
Fresh parsley, tarragon, basil, and chervil,
  shredded with scissors

In a large bowl prepare a marinade by mixing the lemon juice, Tabasco sauce, salt, pepper, oil, and fennel. Marinate the fish for 1 hour in the refrigerator.

Roll the fillets tightly and skewer them, alternating with pieces of tomato and bacon. Season with salt. Brush with melted butter and dip in breadcrumbs. Grill gently for 6 minutes, turning frequently. Season with pepper and sprinkle with herbs. Serve very hot.

149. Tuna Brochettes

Serves 4

150 ml (2/3 cup) dry white wine
Salt, white pepper
4 tbsp olive oil
1 onion, very thinly sliced
2 cloves garlic, crushed
2 shallots, very thinly sliced
Thyme, bay, parsley
600 g (generous 1 1/4 lb) fresh tuna
100 g (3 1/2 oz) bacon, very thinly sliced
4 tomatoes, quartered
2 green peppers, cut into pieces
8 mushrooms, quartered
2 red peppers, cut into pieces
Black olives
Lemon wedges

In a large salad bowl prepare a marinade by mixing the wine, salt, pepper, oil, onion, garlic, shallots, and herbs. Cut the tuna into 2-cm (3/4") cubes. Marinate for 2 hours in a cool place.

Drain the tuna and wrap each piece in a slice of bacon. Secure with a wooden toothpick. Thread onto 4 skewers, alternating tomato, tuna, green pepper, mushroom, tuna, red pepper, and so on. Finish with tomato. Season the brochettes with salt and brush with oil. Grill for 8 minutes over white coals, turning frequently and basting often with the marinade. Serve very hot with the black olives and lemon wedges as garnish.

150. Mixed Fish Brochettes

Serves 4

Juice of 2 limes
Salt, fresh-ground black pepper
1/4 tsp saffron
6 tbsp olive oil
Thyme flowers *or* 1 tsp dried thyme
Fresh rosemary sprigs
Fresh bay leaves
Fillets of sea bass, salmon, *or* mackerel;
   red mullet, tuna, large, shelled shrimp,
   ***or* any other fish or seafood; allow 200 g**
   (scant 1/2 lb) total per person
1 thin slice pork fat *or* bacon per piece of
   fish
4 tomatoes, quartered
4 onions, quartered
Parsley, shredded with scissors
Lime wedges

In a large bowl prepare the marinade by mixing the lime juice, salt, pepper, saffron, oil, thyme, rosemary, and 1 bay leaf. Cut the fish into appropriately sized pieces* and marinate for 1 hour in the refrigerator.

Remove the fish from the marinade and wrap each piece in a slice of pork fat or bacon. Secure with a wooden toothpick. Thread onto 4 skewers, alternating with tomato, half bay leaves, and onion. Brush

*Pieces of tuna should be smaller than pieces of sea bass, for example, because they need more cooking. If you are grilling anything whole, like shrimp, use their size as a base.

the brochettes with oil. Cook for 3 minutes on each side, basting with the marinade from time to time. Season with pepper and sprinkle with a little parsley. Serve with wedges of lime.

151. Lobster Brochettes with Avocado

Serves 4

4 lobster tails, shelled
Juice of 1 lime
75 ml (scant 1/3 cup) olive oil
Salt, oil
Pinch cayenne pepper
Fresh-ground white pepper
1 tbsp Tequila *or* cognac
2 overripe avocados

Cut the lobster tails into 3-cm (1 1/4″) cubes. Prepare the marinade in a crockery bowl. Whisk together the lime juice, oil, a pinch of salt, cayenne, 6 turns of the pepper mill, and Tequila or cognac. Marinate the lobster for 1 hour in a cool place, stirring from time to time. Peel the avocados, cut into large pieces, and sprinkle with lime juice.

Thread the lobster and avocado alternately onto 4 skewers, ending with avocado. Season with salt and brush with oil. Grill for 6 minues, turning often, and baste with the marinade from time to time. Season with pepper before serving.

152. Oyster Brochettes

Serves 4

2 dozen large oysters
24 very thin slices bacon
Cayenne pepper

Shuck the oysters (or have this done when
you buy them) and lay them on a dish towel
or paper towel. Wrap a slice of bacon
around each. Thread 6 oysters onto each
skewer and grill until the bacon is
transparent. Dust with cayenne pepper and
serve on toast.

153. Mussel Brochettes

Serves 4

4 dozen large mussels (have them opened
**   when you buy them)**
48 very thin slices bacon
4 onions, cut into pieces
Fresh-ground white pepper
Lemon wedges

Prepare a bed of coals. Remove the mussels
from their shells and lay them on a dish
towel or paper towel. Wrap a slice of bacon
around each and thread onto skewers
alternately with pieces of onion.

When the coals are white, grill the
brochettes until the bacon begins to drip.
Season with pepper and serve immediately,
garnished with lemon wedges.

154. Scallop Brochettes Émilienne

Serves 4

2 cucumbers
Coarse salt
16 large scallops
Lemon juice
8 paper-thin slices Parma ham
Butter, melted
Fresh-ground white pepper
Fresh parsley, chopped
Lemon wedges

Peel the cucumbers and split them
lengthwise. Remove the seeds from the
centers, then cut each half into pieces 3 cm
(1 1/4") thick. Sprinkle with coarse salt and
set aside for 30 minutes. Cut the scallops in
two horizontally and sprinkle with a few
drops of lemon juice. Cut the slices of ham
in two and wrap a piece around each scallop
half. Secure with wooden toothpicks.

Thread onto 4 skewers, alternating pieces
of cucumber and scallop, ending with
cucumber. Brush the brochettes with
melted butter. Grill for 1 minute on each
side. Season with pepper and sprinkle with
a little chopped parsley. Serve garnished
with lemon wedges.

POULTRY AND GAME

155. Chicken Brochettes with Green Onions

Serves 4

6 tbsp sherry
2 tbsp soy sauce
1 tsp brown sugar
Fresh-ground white pepper
2 boneless chicken breasts, cut into 3-cm (1 1/4″) cubes
8 chicken livers
8 green onions
Peanut oil
Salt

In a crockery bowl prepare the marinade by mixing the sherry, soy sauce, brown sugar, and pepper. Marinate the chicken and livers for 2 hours in a cool place. Cut the green onions into 4-cm (1 1/2″) pieces. Cut the marinated chicken livers in two.

Thread the ingredients onto 4 skewers, alternating chicken, onion, liver, onion, chicken, etc. Brush with oil. Grill for 6 minutes, turning frequently and basting with the marinade at each turn. Season with salt and pepper just before serving.

156. Turkey Brochettes Mexican Style

Serves 4

600 g (generous 1 1/4 lb) breast of young turkey
8 medium onions
8 medium tomatoes
Green bell peppers
Red bell peppers
Salt
Lard, melted
Fresh-ground white pepper

Cut the turkey meat into 3-cm (1 1/4″) cubes. Peel the onions and cut into large pieces. Cut the tomatoes into quarters. Seed the peppers and cut into pieces.

Thread these ingredients onto 4 skewers, alternating tomato, green pepper, turkey, red pepper, onion, and so on, ending with tomato. Season with salt and brush with melted lard. Grill for about 10 minutes, turning frequently and basting with the melted lard from time to time—turkey is by nature a little dry. Season with pepper just before serving.

157. Brochettes Nantaises

Serves 4

**4 boneless duck breasts, about 400 g (scant
  1 lb) each
4 oranges
4 choice eating apples
Lemon juice
Salt
Peanut oil
Green peppercorns, finely crushed**

Cut the duck into 3-cm (1 1/4″) cubes. Peel
the oranges completely with a knife and cut
them into large pieces. Peel the apples and
cut into large chunks; sprinkle with lemon
juice so they do not turn brown.

Thread the ingredients alternately onto
4 skewers. Season with salt and brush with
oil. Grill for about 8 minutes, turning
frequently. The meat should be a little pink
on the inside. Sprinkle with crushed
peppercorns just before serving.

158. Brochettes of Thrushes

Serves 4

**8 plump thrushes* *or* blackbirds *or* snipe
8 juniper berries
8 very thin slices pork fat
12 slices bread
100 g (3 1/2 oz) butter**

Press on the abdomen of each bird to
remove the gizzard and replace it with a
juniper berry. Wrap a sheet of pork fat
around each bird and secure it with string.
Butter the bread and place it in a drip pan so
it can soak up the drippings from the
cooking birds.

Thread 2 birds onto each skewer and
roast for 10 to 12 minutes. Season with salt
and pepper before serving on the bread.

  *Grain farmers would welcome your help in
   getting rid of the blackbirds that rob their
   fields. Use a light load and the finest
   birdshot and look forward to a feast.

PORK

159. West Indian Brochettes

Serves 4

6 oranges
4 limes
4 tbsp peanut oil
**2 pinches thyme flowers *or* small pinch
   dried thyme**
2 pinches paprika
3 shallots, chopped
Hot red pepper, very finely chopped
Fresh-ground black pepper
600 g (generous 1 1/4 lb) pork tenderloin
4 chipolata (cocktail) sausages
2 pork kidneys
Salt, oil

In a crockery bowl whisk thoroughly the
juice of 3 oranges and 2 limes, the oil,
thyme, paprika, shallots, hot pepper, and
black pepper. Cut the pork into 3-cm
(1 1/4") cubes, the chipolatas into 3-cm
(1 1/4") lengths, and the kidneys into
4 pieces. Marinate the meat for 2 hours in a
cool place. Peel 3 oranges and 2 limes
completely with a knife and cut into large
pieces.

   Drain the meat. Thread it and the fruit
alternately onto 4 skewers. Season with salt
and pepper. Brush lightly with oil. Grill for
about 15 minutes, turning often and basting
with marinade at each turn. Serve very hot.

Note: The oranges and limes may
disintegrate during cooking, but they will
have imparted a delightful flavor to the
meat.

160. Pork Brochettes with Armagnac

Serves 4

800 g (1 3/4 lb) lean leg of pork
250 ml (1 cup) olive oil
3 tbsp Armagnac
2 cloves garlic, crushed
1 onion, very finely chopped
Fresh-ground black pepper
Salt

Cut the pork into 3-cm (1 1/4") cubes. In a
large bowl mix the oil, Armagnac, garlic,
onion, and pepper. Marinate the pork for
2 hours in a cool place, stirring from time
to time.

   Drain the meat. Thread onto 4 skewers
and grill gently for about 20 minutes,
sprinkling occasionally with marinade.
Season with salt and pepper. Serve very hot.

161. Southeast Asian Brochettes

Serves 4

1 tsp brown sugar
1 tsp finely minced fresh ginger *or* pinch
   dried ginger
100 ml (1/3 cup) soy sauce
300 ml (1 1/3 cups) Chinese shao-shing wine
   or sherry
4 tbsp peanut oil
Fresh-ground black pepper
800 g (1 3/4 lb) lean, boneless pork
2 red bell peppers, seeded and cut into
   pieces
4 slices fresh pineapple, cut into pieces
2 onions, cut into pieces
Salt, oil

In a large bowl mix the brown sugar, ginger,
soy sauce, and Chinese wine or sherry. Add
the oil and pepper. Cut the pork fillet into
2-cm (3/4″) cubes and marinate for 2 hours
in a cool place.

Drain the pork and thread onto 4
skewers, alternating it with the red pepper,
pineapple, and onion. Season with salt and
pepper. Brush with oil. Grill over a
moderate fire for about 15 minutes, turning
frequently and sprinkling with the marinade
from time to time.

162. Black and White Brochettes

Serves 4

400 g (good 3/4 lb) blood sausage
400 g (good 3/4 lb) white sausage *or*
   pork sausage
2 choice eating apples
2 onions
Lemon juice
Fresh-ground nutmeg
200 g (scant 1/2 lb) fat bacon
Salt, white pepper
Butter, melted

Cut the sausages into 4-cm (1 1/2″) slices.
Peel the apples and onions and cut into large
pieces. Sprinkle lemon juice over the
apples, then the nutmeg.

Thread onto 4 skewers, alternating
bacon, onion, blood sausage, apple, white
sausage, apple, and so on. (Thread the
sausage slices sideways, through the skins.)
Season with salt and pepper and dip in
melted butter. Grill gently for about
15 minutes, turning once.

VEAL

163. Veal Brochettes with Eggplant

Serves 4

**600 g (generous 1 1/4 lb) boneless loin of
  veal**
200 g (scant 1/2 lb) fat bacon, unsliced
3 very small eggplants
Lemon juice
Olive oil
Breadcrumbs
Salt, white pepper
Fresh chives, snipped small with scissors

Cut the veal and bacon into similar-sized
pieces, about 2 cm (3/4"). Peel the eggplants
and cut into 2-cm (3/4") cubes. Sprinkle
with lemon juice.

   Thread the veal, bacon, and eggplant
alternately onto 4 skewers. Brush the
brochettes with oil and dip in breadcrumbs.
Grill for 5 minutes on each side. Season with
salt and pepper. Sprinkle lightly with chives
before serving.

164. Veal Boulettes with Sage

Serves 4

200 g (7 oz) breadcrumbs
Little milk, warmed
10 leaves fresh sage, finely chopped, *or*
  1 tbsp dried sage
3 leaves fresh mint, finely chopped, *or*
  1 tsp dried mint
800 g (1 3/4 lb) lean veal, finely chopped
2 egg yolks
Juice of 1 lemon
Salt, white pepper, nutmeg
12 leaves fresh sage
Olive oil

Soak the breadcrumbs in the milk. Squeeze
dry and put into a mixing bowl with the
chopped sage, mint, ground veal, egg yolks,
lemon juice, salt, pepper, and nutmeg.
Knead thoroughly.

   Form into 16 round balls. Thread them 4
to a skewer, separated by the sage leaves.
Brush with oil. Grill for 5 minutes on each
side.

BEEF

165. Brochettes of Beef with Artichokes

Serves 4

800 g (1 3/4 lb) beef tenderloin
Fresh-ground white pepper
8 artichoke hearts, blanched for 2 minutes
  in salted water with lemon juice added
Butter, melted
Breadcrumbs
Salt

Cut the meat into 3-cm (1 1/4″) cubes. Season with pepper. Cut the artichoke hearts into as many pieces as you have pieces of meat, plus 4.

Thread the artichokes and meat alternately onto 4 skewers, beginning and ending with artichokes. Brush the brochettes with melted butter and dip in breadcrumbs. Cook for 5 minutes on a hot grill, turning once. Season with salt before serving.

166. Jouquard Brochettes

Serves 4

800 g (1 3/4 lb) top round *or* sirloin tip
Celery
Red peppers
Onions
Large green olives, stuffed with anchovies
White pepper
Olive oil
Salt

Cut the steak into 2-cm (3/4″) cubes. Cut the celery and peppers into 2-cm (3/4″) squares and quarter the onions.

Thread the meat and vegetables onto 4 skewers, alternating the peppers, celery, meat, olives, and onions. Season with pepper and brush with oil. Grill for 6 minutes, turning once. Season with salt before serving.

167. Portuguese Brochettes

Serves 4

**800 g (1 3/4 lb) well-trimmed shell of
 beef* *or* 4 T-bone steaks, 3 cm (1 1/4″)
 thick
200 ml (scant 1 cup) Madeira *or* medium
 dry sherry
100 ml (1/3 cup) red wine vinegar
2 cloves garlic, crushed
10 white peppercorns
2 bay leaves
Olive oil
Salt, white pepper**

If you are using T-bone steaks, discard the
"tails" and all bone and gristle. Cut the
lean meat into 3-cm (1 1/4″) cubes and place
in a bowl. Mix the Madeira or sherry,
vinegar, garlic, peppercorns, and bay leaves
and pour over the meat. Cover and let stand
in a cool place for 2 days.

On the day of the barbecue drain the
meat, pat dry in a clean dish towel, and
thread onto 4 skewers. Brush lightly with
oil. Grill for 4 minutes, turning often.
Season with salt and pepper just before
serving.

 *In French, *contre-filet*—the meat opposite
 (on the other side of the bone from) the
 tenderloin or *filet*. This cut is not always
 available from North American butchers;
 when it is, it may be called *club*, *striploin*,
 or *New York cut*.

168. Mexican Rolls

Serves 4

**1 ripe avocado
2 large tomatoes, peeled, seeded, and
 crushed
Juice of 1 lime
2 shallots, finely chopped
Salt, fresh-ground white pepper
3 tbsp olive oil
Dash Tabasco sauce
8 very thin slices round steak, about 80 g
 (3 oz) each**

Prepare the Mexican sauce by blending
together the avocado and tomato pulp.
When the mixture is smooth, add the lime
juice, shallots, salt, and pepper. Whisk. Add
the oil a drop at a time, then the Tabasco
sauce.

Oil the steaks lightly and season with
pepper on both sides. Roll them up tightly,
pinning the rolls with the skewers. Grill
for 3 minutes. Serve immediately with a
bowl of the Mexican sauce.

LAMB

169. Shashlik

Serves 4

**400 g (scant 1 lb) lean shoulder *or* leg of
   lamb
4 lamb kidneys
4 chipolata (cocktail) sausages
50 ml (scant 1/4 cup) olive oil
Lemon juice
50 ml (scant 1/4 cup) vodka
Fresh-ground white pepper
Thyme, bay leaf
4 small tomatoes
Salt**

Cut all the meat into 3-cm (1 1/4″) cubes.
Make up a marinade by mixing the oil,
lemon juice, vodka, pepper, thyme, and
bay leaf in a large bowl. Add the meat and
marinate for 2 hours in a cool place.

   Heat the barbecue. Split the kidneys
almost, but not quite, in two. Thread the
meat onto 4 skewers, alternating lamb,
kidney, and chipolata and ending with a
tomato. Grill for 3 minutes on each side.
Season with salt before serving.

Note: The Russian way to serve shashlik is
on the skewers, sprinkled with vodka and
flambéed.

170. Lamb Brochettes with Lime

Serves 4

**600 g (generous 1 1/4 lb) leg of lamb,
   completely lean
Juice of 7 limes
Fresh-ground white pepper
2 small hot red peppers, finely chopped
500 g (1 lb) onions, thinly sliced
Olive oil
Fresh tarragon, shredded with scissors
Salt**

Cut the lamb into 3-cm (1 1/4″) cubes. Leave
to marinate for 2 hours in a cool place in the
lime juice, pepper, hot peppers, and onions.

   Drain and wipe the meat. Thread onto 4
skewers and brush with oil. Grill for 6
minutes, turning often and sprinkling from
time to time with a few drops of the
marinade. Sprinkle with a little tarragon and
season with salt just as the dish is served.

171. Djerba Brochettes

Serves 6

800 g (1 3/4 lb) lean lamb
Lamb fat (preferably kidney fat)
18 small onions
Salt, white pepper
Powdered savory and sage
6 pieces baguette (long French bread), split
**   in two horizontally**

Cut the lamb meat and fat into 3-cm (1 1/4″)
cubes. Thread onto 6 skewers, alternating
lamb, fat, and onions. Season generously
with salt and pepper. Dust with savory and
sage.

   Grill for 6 minutes, turning often. Every
time you turn the brochettes, press them
firmly into the pieces of bread. Serve the
brochettes well done and in the hollows of
the bread that is by now soaked in the
cooking juices.

172. Kurdish Brochettes

Serves 4

800 g (1 3/4 lb) lean leg of lamb
Juice of 3 onions
Juice of 1 lemon
Salt, white pepper
Olive oil
Handful almonds, toasted and slivered
Sour cream

Cut the lamb into 3-cm (1 1/4'') cubes.
Marinate for 2 hours in a cool place in the
onion juice, lemon juice, salt, and pepper.

   Drain the meat well and thread onto
4 skewers. Brush with oil. Cook over
whitening coals for 4 or 5 minutes, turning
often. Remove the kebabs from the skewers
and arrange on a hot platter. Scatter the
almonds over the meat and pour over the
sour cream.

173. Madras Brochettes

Serves 4

800 g (1 3/4 lb) shoulder of lamb
200 ml (scant 1 cup) sesame oil
2 tbsp *cari rose* (ideal for grilling) *or* mild
   curry powder
Juice of 1 lemon
1 clove garlic, crushed
Salt
Coconut, grated
Fresh mint leaves

Cut the lamb into 3-cm (1 1/4") cubes. Marinate in a cool place for 2 hours in the oil, *cari rose* or curry powder, lemon juice, and garlic.

   Drain the meat and dry on a paper towel. Thread onto 4 skewers and grill for 6 minutes, turning often. Sprinkle with marinade from time to time. Season with salt just before serving and sprinkle lightly with coconut. Serve very hot, garnished with mint leaves.

174. Boulettes of Lamb en Brochettes

Serves 4

800 g (1 3/4 lb) lean lamb, ground
2 tbsp breadcrumbs
1 clove garlic, minced or finely mashed
1 egg, beaten
Salt, white pepper
1 red bell pepper
1 green bell pepper
Olive oil

Mix together the ground meat, breadcrumbs, garlic, egg, salt, and pepper. Form the mixture into 16 round balls by rolling the mixture between your palms. Cut the peppers into 3-cm (1 1/4") squares. Brush with oil.

   Thread the boulettes onto 4 skewers, alternating with pieces of pepper. Brush with oil and grill for 8 minutes, turning often.

ORGAN MEAT

175. Chicken Liver Brochettes with Verveine du Velay

Serves 4

600 g (generous 1 1/4 lb) chicken livers
100 ml (1/3 cup) Verveine du Velay *or* other herb liqueur
1 shallot, chopped
2 sprigs fresh thyme *or* 2 tbsp dried thyme
1 bay leaf
Fresh-ground white pepper
200 g (scant 1/2 lb) streaky bacon
250 g (1/2 lb) small mushrooms
Salt
Butter, melted
Breadcrumbs
Fresh parsley, shredded with scissors

In a crockery bowl marinate the livers in the herb liqueur, shallot, thyme, bay leaf, and pepper. Set aside in a cool place for 1 hour. Cut the bacon into squares. Clean the mushrooms, discarding the stems. Drain the livers and cut them in two.

Thread the liver, bacon, and mushrooms alternately onto 4 skewers. Season with salt and pepper. Dip each brochette into melted butter and then into breadcrumbs. Grill gently for 6 minutes, turning frequently. Serve hot, sprinkled lightly with parsley.

176. Veal Hearts Santiago

Serves 4

2 veal hearts
2 cloves garlic, crushed
2 bell peppers, red and green, thinly sliced
100 ml (1/3 cup) plus 1 tbsp vinegar
Salt
200 ml (3/4 cup) olive oil
Juice of 1 lime
2 onions, very finely chopped
1 hot red pepper, finely chopped

Soak the veal hearts well in cold water. Drain, cut open, and remove all gristle and "strings." Cut into 3-cm (1 1/4") cubes and place in a mixing bowl. Add the garlic, bell peppers, 100 ml (1/3 cup) vinegar, and salt. Cover and marinate in a cool place overnight.

Drain the meat and pat dry. Thread onto 4 skewers and roast directly over the coals for about 8 minutes. While the brochettes are cooking, prepare a sauce by mixing the oil, 1 tbsp vinegar, lime juice, onions, and hot pepper. Season the brochettes with salt and serve with this sauce.

177. Veal Giblet Brochettes

Serves 4

2 slices calf's liver
2 veal sweetbreads, ready to cook*
2 veal kidneys
16 slices bacon
6 tbsp olive oil
2 bay leaves, crumbled
1 tbsp thyme flowers *or* 1 tsp dried thyme
Fresh-ground white pepper
Bay leaves, halved
Salt
Fresh basil, shredded with scissors

Cut the liver, sweetbreads, and kidneys into 3-cm (1 1/4″) cubes, the bacon into 3-cm (1 1/4″) pieces. Mix the oil, crumbled bay leaves, thyme, and pepper in a mixing bowl. Marinate all the meat for 15 minutes.

Drain the meat and thread onto 4 skewers, alternating bacon, sweetbread, half bay leaf, kidney, bacon, half bay leaf, liver, and so on, ending with bacon. Grill for 4 minutes on each side. Season with salt and pepper. Sprinkle with basil before serving.

*Sweetbreads are often sold ready to cook. If not, soak them for 30 minutes in cold water, then drain and carefully remove all veins and membranes. Simmer them in fresh water for 15 minutes with 1 tsp salt and 1 tsp lemon juice per liter (quart) of water. (Save the cooking water for stock.)

178. Lamb Kidney Shish Kebabs

Serves 4

16 lamb kidneys
4 firm tomatoes
Green bell peppers
Salt, white pepper
Olive oil
Onions, very finely chopped
Powdered coriander

Split the kidneys in two and thread onto 4 skewers alternately with pieces of tomato and green pepper. Season with salt and pepper and brush with oil. Roll in the onions dusted with coriander. Grill for 4 minutes, turning often.

Note: You can make authentic shish kebabs by replacing the kidneys with 800 g (1 3/4 lb) shoulder of lamb cut into 3-cm (1 1/4″) cubes and grilling for 6 minutes.

MIXED BROCHETTES

179. Brochettes Dubrovnik

Serves 4

400 g (scant 1 lb) leg of pork
400 g (scant 1 lb) center-cut leg of veal
4 large white onions
Salt, fresh-ground white pepper
Olive oil
Paprika
4 large red onions, coarsely chopped

Cut the meat into 3-cm (1 1/4″) cubes. Cut the white onions into large pieces.

Thread onto 4 skewers, alternating onion, pork, onion, veal, onion, and so on. Season with salt and pepper and brush with olive oil. Grill for about 15 minutes, turning once. Serve very hot, dusted with paprika, on a bed of the red onions.

180. Brochette Medley

Per person

50 g (1 3/4 oz) beef tenderloin
50 g (1 3/4 oz) lamb loin (after boning and trimming)
50 g (1 3/4 oz) center-cut leg of veal
1 chipolata (cocktail) sausage, cut in three
1 lamb kidney, split 3 times and spread flat
5 pieces bacon
1 mushroom, halved
1 tomato, quartered
Fresh-ground white pepper
Olive oil
Salt
Maître d'hôtel butter (Receipe 17)

Place the meat, mushroom, and tomato in a mixing bowl; season with pepper and sprinkle with oil. Mix together with your hands to be sure that the meat and vegetables are well coated with oil and seasoning.

Thread everything onto skewers in a regularly alternating pattern, beginning and ending with pieces of tomato. Grill for 8 minutes, turning once. Season with salt and pepper near the end of the cooking time. Serve very hot, with a knob of maître d'hôtel butter in the center of the kidney.

VEGETABLES

181. Brochettes of Baby Artichokes

Serves 4

16 small, very young, and very tender artichokes*
4 large, firm tomatoes *or* **16 cherry tomatoes**
Bay leaves, halved
Olive oil
Salt, fresh-ground white pepper
Lemon juice

Clean the artichokes, removing the outer leaves and stems. If you are using large tomatoes, cut them into quarters.

Thread onto 4 skewers, alternating tomato, artichoke, half bay leaf, and so on. Brush with olive oil. Grill for 12 minutes, turning often. Salt halfway through. Season with pepper and sprinkle with lemon juice before serving.

*In France these are known as artichokes *poivrades*; in Provence they are called *mourre-de-cat*.

182. Marinated Mushroom Brochettes

Serves 4

500 g (generous 1 lb) medium-sized mushrooms
Juice of 1 lemon
200 ml (scant 1 cup) olive oil
500 ml (2 cups) dry white wine
Salt, fresh-ground white pepper
2 tbsp chopped fresh coriander *or* **2 tsp dried coriander**
Bay leaf
2 tbsp chopped fresh fennel *or* **2 tsp dried fennel**
200 g (scant 1/2 lb) thinly sliced bacon
Paprika

Brush the mushrooms clean and discard the stems. Marinate for 2 hours in a cool place in a mixture of the lemon juice, oil, wine, salt, pepper, coriander, bay leaf, and fennel.

Drain the mushrooms and wrap each in a slice of bacon. Secure with a wooden toothpick. Thread onto 4 skewers and grill for about 10 minutes, turning often. Dust with paprika before serving.

183. Garden Brochettes

Serves 4

1 eggplant
Coarse salt
1 red bell pepper
1 green bell pepper
2 large, *or* 8 small, firm tomatoes
2 large onions *or* 8 green onions
8 heads red chicory*
Olive oil
Salt, fresh-ground white pepper

Peel the eggplant and cut into large cubes. Sprinkle with coarse salt and set aside for 30 minutes. Cut the peppers into rectangular pieces and the tomatoes and onions into quarters if you are using large ones. Trim the chicory.

Drain the eggplant. Thread the vegetables alternately onto 4 skewers and brush with oil. Grill for about 15 minutes, turning often. Add salt halfway through cooking. Season with pepper just before serving.

*If not available, replace with an endive or a small squash.

184. Ratatouille Brochettes

Serves 4

2 very small eggplants
Juice of 1 lemon
6 tbsp olive oil
1 onion, chopped
2 cloves garlic, crushed
Thyme flowers *or* dried thyme
Salt, fresh-ground white pepper
1 red bell pepper
1 green bell pepper
4 small zucchini
8 small, firm tomatoes
Green and black olives

Peel the eggplants and cut into large cubes. Leave to soak for 1 hour in a cool place in a mixture of the lemon juice, oil, onion, garlic, thyme, salt, and pepper. Stir from time to time. Cut the peppers into rectangular pieces and the zucchini into large cubes (don't peel them).

Drain the eggplant and thread all the vegetables alternately onto 4 skewers. Brush with the marinade. Grill for 5 minutes, turning often and basting from time to time with the marinade. Add salt halfway through cooking. Season with pepper before serving. Serve garnished with green and black olives.

CHEESE AND FRUIT

185. Cheddar Brochettes in Five Flavors

Serves 4

1 kg (2 1/4 lb) cheddar *or* other firm cheese
5 separate 50-ml (scant 1/4-cup) glasses peanut oil
1 tbsp paprika
1 tbsp curry powder
1 tbsp chopped garlic
8 very thin slices lean bacon
50 ml (scant 1/4 cup) cognac
Fresh-ground white pepper

The day before the barbecue mix each glass of oil with one of the flavorings —one with the paprika, one with the curry powder, one with the garlic, one with the bacon, and the last with the cognac. Cut the cheddar into 2-cm (3/4″) cubes. Divide the cubes into 5 equal portions and set each portion to marinate overnight in one of the flavored oils.

The next day thread the cheese onto 4 skewers, alternating the flavors. Wrap the pieces marinated in the bacon oil with the bacon slices. Grill just until the cheese begins to melt. Season with pepper and eat immediately.

186. Fruit Brochettes

Serves 8

1 fresh pineapple, peeled and cut into small pieces
4 bananas, peeled and cut in four
8 apricots, halved
4 plums, halved
4 pears, peeled and cut into large pieces
Juice of 2 oranges
Juice of 1 lemon
4 tbsp dark rum
200 g (7 oz) granulated sugar

Place all the fruit in a mixing bowl and sprinkle with the orange juice, lemon juice, rum, and sugar. Mix carefully. Thread onto 8 skewers, alternating the fruits. Grill over a hot fire until the sugar caramelizes.

You can also serve these brochettes flambéed with rum.

VIII
Spit Roasts

FISH AND SEAFOOD

187. Spit-Roasted Salmon

Serves 12–15

1 whole salmon, about 5 kg (11 lb)
500 g (generous 1 lb) sweet butter
Salt, white pepper
150 g (5 oz) chopped fresh dill *or*
   40 g (1 1/2 oz) dried dill
Oil
Anchovy butter (Recipe 9)

Remove the gills and clean the fish through this opening, without cutting into the abdomen. Rinse and drain well. Work the salt, pepper, and dill into the butter and stuff the fish with this. Brush the salmon with oil and wrap it in aluminum foil.

   Place the fish on a spit and let it turn over the fire for about 45 minutes. It should remain moist on the inside. Serve with anchovy butter.

188. Spit-Roasted Tuna

Serves 4

1 kg (2 1/4 lb) piece fresh tuna *or* **bonito**
   (type of skipjack)
250 ml (1 cup) olive oil
Juice of 1 lemon
Bouquet garni
1 sprig fresh basil *or* **1 tsp dried basil**
2 cloves garlic, crushed
Salt, white pepper

Marinate the tuna in the other ingredients for 2 hours in a cool place. Turn often. Place on a spit and let it turn over the fire for about 20 minutes, basting frequently with the marinade.

189. Spit-Roasted Lobster

Per person

1 lobster, about 800 g (1 3/4 lb)
Oil
Shallot butter (Recipe 10)

Scald the lobster for 2 minutes in salted water. Place it on a spit and let it turn over the fire for 12 minutes, sprinkling with oil from time to time. Serve with shallot butter.

POULTRY AND GAME

190. Spit-Roasted Chicken

Serves 4

75 g (2 3/4 oz) butter
2 tbsp chopped fresh tarragon *or* 2 tsp
dried tarragon
Salt, white pepper
1 large, first-quality, free-range chicken
Butter
Water
Juice of 1 lemon
1 tbsp thick cream *or* 35% cream, such as
whipping cream

Work the tarragon into the butter and season with salt and pepper. Stuff the chicken with this and truss it for roasting.* Butter the outside. Pour 1 cm (3/8″) water and the lemon juice into the drip pan.

Place the chicken on a spit and let it turn for 20 minutes per 500 g (1 lb) over a good fire. Don't add salt, and baste only during the first three-quarters of the cooking time; then add the cream to the drippings in the pan. To test that the chicken is cooked, pierce the thickest part of the thigh with a skewer; a clear juice should run out. Carve the chicken. Serve the pan gravy separately.

*Tie the legs and wings firmly to the body with string so the bird holds its shape during cooking.

191. Duck with Fruit

Serves 4

1 duck, 2 kg (4 1/2 lb), trussed*
Salt, white pepper
Orange and lemon zest
Half a lemon
300 ml (1 1/3 cups) dry cider
4 firm peaches, peeled and quartered
4 choice eating apples, quartered and
**   sprinkled with lemon juice**
2 oranges, peeled completely with a knife,
**   quartered, and soaked in a little**
**   Curaçao**

Dust the duck cavity with salt and pepper and place the orange and lemon zest inside. Rub the outside with lemon. Pour the cider into the drip pan.

Roast the duck on a spit for 40 minutes, basting every 5 minutes with the contents of the drip pan. Add the peach and apple quarters to the drip pan 10 minutes before the duck is cooked and stop basting at this time so that the skin becomes crisp. Let the duck rest for 10 minutes in a warm place before carving. Serve the carved meat garnished with peach, apple, and orange quarters. Pour the strained pan gravy over it as well as the Curaçao in which the oranges were soaked. Season with salt and pepper.

*See note to Recipe 190.

192. Spit-Roasted Goose

Serves 6

1 goose liver, chopped
200 g (scant 1/2 lb) lean pork, chopped
100 g (3 1/2 oz) butter, softened
3 eggs, beaten
2 shallots, chopped
1 clove garlic, minced or well mashed
1 stem fresh basil *or* 1 tbsp dried basil
4 leaves fresh sage, chopped, *or* 1 tsp dried
**   sage**
Handful breadcrumbs, soaked in milk and
**   squeezed dry**
Salt, white peppe
Nutmeg
1 young goose, 2.5 kg (5 1/2 lb)
Butter, melted
2 tbsp prepared hot mustard
Dry breadcrumbs
100 ml (1/3 cup) dry white wine
Juice of 1 lemon

Prepare a stuffing by mixing together the liver, pork, softened butter, eggs, shallots, garlic, herbs, soaked breadcrumbs, salt, pepper, and nutmeg. Stuff and truss* the goose. Brush lightly with melted butter. Pour any remaining melted butter into the drip pan.

*See note to Recipe 190.

Roast the goose on a spit over a hot fire for 1 hour, turning it and basting from time to time with the juice from the drip pan. After an hour mix half the mustard into the drippings in the pan. Baste the goose with this mixture and spread it with breadcrumbs. Repeat until the goose is completely coated. Cook for a further 30 minutes.

Pour off the fat from the drip pan, then add the wine, lemon juice, and the remaining mustard; mix vigorously. Season the gravy with salt and pepper and serve separately.

193. Spit-Roasted Pheasant

Serves 2

75 g (2 3/4 oz) butter
Salt, white pepper
1 pheasant, including the liver
Thick bard*
"Country" bread (domed, round loaf of
  coarse bread)
60 ml (1/4 cup) port

Work salt and pepper into the butter and place in the cavity of the pheasant. Wrap the pheasant in the bard and secure it with string. In a very hot frying pan sauté the pheasant liver in butter; season with salt and pepper. Butter both sides of a large, thick slice of bread and toast both sides on the grill. Keep the liver and grilled bread warm.

Roast the pheasant on a spit for 45 minutes. Ten minutes before cooking is complete, remove the bard so that the skin browns well. Empty the gravy from inside the bird into the drip pan and keep hot. Add the port. Crush the liver in a little of the drippings, spread this on the slice of grilled bread, and cut the bread into 4 croutons.

Carve the pheasant and serve with pan gravy spooned over it and garnished with croutons.

*A sheet of pork fat large enough to wrap around the pheasant and about 2 cm (3/4") thick. In France the crisp bard is often served with game birds; it's too good to throw away!

194. Spit-Roasted Hare

Serves 4

1 young hare,* finely larded**
Salt, white pepper
250 ml (1 cup) full-bodied red wine
60 ml (1/4 cup) cognac
Onion and shallot, chopped
Orange zest
Savory
Butter
Small chunks pork fat
200 ml (scant 1 cup) thick cream *or* 35%
   cream, such as whipping cream

Rub the hare with salt and pepper. Marinate
for 12 hours in a cool place in the wine,
cognac, onion, shallot, orange zest, and
savory. Turn often. In the meantime, fasten
a metal funnel firmly to the end of a stick.
While the hare is roasting, heat the funnel
red hot and drop chunks of pork fat into it;
the fat will melt, and you can baste the hare
with it.

   Wipe the hare dry and place it on a spit.
Pour the marinade into the drip pan with a
large knob of butter. Roast the hare for
40 minutes, basting the shoulders and
haunches with boiling fat from the funnel
and basting it all with the marinade every 10
minutes. When the hare is done, mix the
thick cream into the drippings in the pan.
Carve the hare and serve with the strained
gravy poured over top.

*The western jackrabbit and the northern
snowshoe hare are the only North
American hares. They are similar to rabbits,
but much larger, and their meat is both
tougher and much more flavorful than that
of domestic rabbits sold by butchers.
Possible substitutes for hare in this recipe
might be wild rabbit, gray or black squirrel,
or young woodchuck or beaver. Adjust the
cooking times and number of persons
served according to the size of the animal
used; remove all traces of natural fat from
woodchuck and beaver before cooking.

**Using a larding needle, ''stitch'' thin strips
of pork fat through the meat at regular
intervals. Some butchers will do this for
you. Meat deficient in natural fat is usually
larded. Lardoons for a lean roast of beef
might be as wide as 2 cm (3/4"), but for
hare they should be much thinner.

195. Spit-Roasted Haunch of Caribou

Serves 12

1 haunch young caribou,* skinned,
   larded,** and with the hip bone
   removed
Salt, white pepper
Butter, melted
1.5 liters (6 1/2 cups or 2 bottles) dry white
   wine
2 kg (4 1/2 lb) cooked chestnuts *or* canned
   chestnuts, drained

6 tbsp thick cream *or* **35% cream, such as whipping cream**
Fresh, unsalted butter
Nutmeg

Rub the caribou haunch with salt and pepper. Sprinkle with melted butter. Pour half the wine into the drip pan.

Place the haunch on a spit and roast for 30 minutes per kg (2 1/4 lb), basting often with the contents of the drip pan. Add the remaining wine to the pan 10 minutes before cooking is complete; do not baste again. Reheat the chestnuts in the drip pan. Remove with a skimmer and blend into a puree with the cream and butter. Adjust the seasoning with salt, pepper, and nutmeg. Carve the roast and serve it with its pan gravy and the chestnut puree on the side.

  *This recipe was designed for the roebuck (*chevreuil*), which is known only in Europe and parts of Asia. Fortunately, the Canadian caribou, although somewhat larger, is very similar in taste and method of cooking: young roebuck and caribou are the only 2 sorts of venison that need neither aging nor marinating. This recipe has been adjusted accordingly.

  **Using a larding needle, "stitch" thin strips of pork fat, about 1 cm (3/8") wide, through the meat at intervals of 6 cm (2 1/2") or so. Some butchers will do this for you.

196. Spit-Roasted Haunch of Young Wild Boar

Serves 12

1 haunch young wild boar,* skinned and larded **
1 bottle white wine (or more)
Carrots, thinly sliced
Onions, thinly sliced
Shallots, thinly sliced
Thyme, bay leaf, parsley
Allspice
Black peppercorns
60 ml (1/4 cup) cognac *or* **brandy**
Butter, melted
Salt

In a nonmetallic container just large enough to hold the haunch, prepare a marinade with the wine, sliced vegetables, herbs, spices, and cognac or brandy. Marinate for 48 hours in a very cool place. There must be enough marinade to cover the meat.

Drain and dry the meat and brush with melted butter. Place the haunch on a spit and roast for 40 minutes per kg (2 1/4 lb), basting every 10 minutes with a little marinade and the drippings from the pan. Season with salt when half cooked.

Serve with blueberry or cranberry jelly and applesauce lightly flavored with cinnamon.

  *Available from some specialty butchers, particularly in California.

  **See note 2 to Recipe 195.

PORK

197. Spit-Roasted Loin of Pork

Serves 8

**1 pork loin roast, cut from the "thick end,"
about 2 kg (4 1/2 lb), with a 1-cm (3/8″)
layer of fat
200 g (7 oz) coarse salt
250 ml (1 cup) water
16 cloves garlic, not peeled
Fresh-ground black pepper**

Rub the roast with coarse salt and set aside
for 2 hours in a cool place, turning often.
Carefully wipe the meat clean and place it
on a spit. Pour half the water into the drip
pan.

Roast the pork for 1 1/4 hours, basting
every 5 minutes. After 45 minutes put the
garlic into the drip pan with the remaining
water. Carve the roast and sprinkle the meat
with black pepper. Garlic lovers can also
squeeze the cloves of garlic over the meat.

198. Spit-Roasted Leg of Pork

Serves 15

**1 leg of pork, about 4 kg (9 lb)
2 bottles full-bodied red wine
100 ml (1/3 cup) olive oil
Large bouquet garni
10 juniper berries
10 black peppercorns
2 carrots, very thinly sliced
2 cloves garlic, crushed
2 onions, very thinly sliced
Salt**

In a nonmetallic container just large enough
to hold the roast prepare the marinade with
all the ingredients. Marinate the meat for 24
hours in a cool place.

Place the roast on a spit and turn over a
medium fire for 3 hours. Then remove the
rind, season the fat well with salt, and roast
the meat for 1 more hour. Baste frequently
with the marinade during the entire cooking
time. This dish is traditionally enjoyed with
pears cooked in white wine and with an
assortment of chutneys.

VEAL

199. Spit-Roasted Loin of Veal

Serves 6

**2 kg (4 1/2 lb) veal loin (with kidney),
  larded***
Juice of 2 oranges
Juice of 1 lemon
2 onions, very thinly sliced
**4 stalks fresh coriander *or* 4 tbsp dried
  coriander**
1 stalk fresh sage *or* 1 tbsp dried sage
1 tsp whole allspice
Fresh-ground white pepper
12 broccoli florets
12 small new potatoes
Olive oil
Salt
1 tbsp Curaçao
1 tbsp arrowroot *or* cornstarch

Marinate the veal for 4 hours in the juice of 1
orange, the lemon juice, onions, coriander,
sage, allspice, and pepper. Turn every 30
minutes. Wrap the broccoli and potatoes,
sprinkled with oil, salt, and pepper, in
aluminum foil. (Make several small packets.)

Pour the marinade into the drip pan. Place
the roast on a spit and turn over a medium
fire for 1 1/2 hours. Baste every 10 minutes
with the marinade. Season with salt when
half cooked. Place the foil-wrapped
vegetables on the coals 1 hour before the
veal is done.

Combine the juice of the second orange
with the Curaçao; dissolve in this the
arrowroot or cornstarch. Stir this into the
pan drippings; stir briskly until it thickens.
Serve the gravy over the carved veal.
Garnish with the vegetables.

*See note 2 to Recipe 195.

BEEF

200. Spit-Roasted Beef Tenderloin

Serves 6

1.5 kg (scant 3 1/4 lb) beef tenderloin
Fresh-ground white pepper
100 ml (1/3 cup) olive oil
Juice of 2 lemons
Maître d'hôtel butter (Recipe 17)

Rub the beef with pepper and brush it with
a mixture of oil and lemon juice. Wrap in
aluminum foil and set aside in a cool place
overnight.

   Wipe the meat lightly, place it on a spit,
and roast for 20 to 25 minutes. Remove
from the spit and let stand in a warm place
for 10 minutes before carving to allow the
meat to "set." Carve into thick slices.
Season each serving with salt and pepper.
Serve with maître d'hôtel butter.

201. Spit-Roasted Beef Tongue

Serves 6

1 beef tongue, about 1.5 kg (scant 3 1/4 lb),
   blanched, skinned, and trimmed
1 onion, very finely chopped
1 tbsp prepared hot mustard
3 tbsp fresh basil, shredded with scissors,
   or 3 tsp dried basil
Salt, fresh-ground white pepper
2 tbsp vinegar
3 tbsp butter, melted

Mix the onion, mustard, basil, salt, pepper,
and 1 tbsp vinegar thoroughly. Coat the
beef tongue with half of this mixture. Pour
the rest into the drip pan with the remaining
vinegar and the melted butter.

   Place the tongue on a spit and turn over
whitening coals for 35 minutes, basting
frequently. Serve with a cucumber salad.

202. Spit-Roasted Contre-Filet

Serves 6

1 shell of beef,* 1.8 kg (4 lb)
Fresh-ground white pepper
Pork bards**
Hot water
1 onion, quartered
1 carrot, cut into rounds
Salt

Season the meat generously with pepper, wrap in the bards, and secure them with string. Put a little hot water into a drip pan along with the onion and carrot.

Place the roast on a spit and turn over a hot fire for no longer than 30 minutes. Season with salt after 15 minutes. Allow the roast to rest in a warm place for 10 minutes before carving. Strain the pan gravy and add the juices from the carving platter. Season with salt and pepper if necessary and pour this gravy over the carved meat.

 *See note to Recipe 166.
**Thin sheets of pork fat, about 1–1.5 cm (3/8–3/4″) thick and as large as possible, used to protect delicate or lean meats during roasting and to prevent the surface from drying or hardening. Your butcher may have to cut it to order for you.

LAMB AND GOAT

203. Spit-Roasted Leg of Lamb

Serves 6

1 leg of lamb, about 2.5 kg (5 1/2 lb)
1 clove garlic, peeled
Butter
250 ml (1 cup) dry white wine
Fresh rosemary *or* dried rosemary
Salt, white pepper
Lemon wedges
1 bud garlic

Slip a clove of garlic between the meat and the bone at the thickest part of the leg. Place the leg on a spit and butter the surfaces. Place the wine, rosemary, salt, pepper, lemon, and garlic bud in the drip pan.

Let the lamb turn for 1 hour, basting with the contents of the drip pan every 5 minutes. Allow the roast to rest for 10 minutes, then carve into thin slices.

204. Méchoui*

1 whole lamb, about 15 kg (33 lb),
**   including the kidneys**
Salt, fresh-ground white pepper
Garlic salt
Ground thyme, wild thyme, bay leaves,
**   and rosemary**
500 g (generous 1 lb) butter
150 g (5 oz) margarine
250 ml (1 cup) olive oil

Dig a trench 1.5 m (5′) long by 0.5 m (over 1 1/2′) wide and 0.4 m (nearly 1 1/2′) deep. Drive stakes into the ground close to 1 side of the trench to support the ends of the spit. Prepare the bed of coals in this trench at least 2 hours in advance, using 20 to 25 kg (about 50 lb) of charcoal.

Méchoui is Arabic for "roast." European travellers encountered the word when they were honored in traditional Bedouin style by the slaughter of a young lamb, and so *méchoui* passed into the European languages to mean this festive outdoor barbecue of a whole lamb.

Coat the lamb generously inside and out
with a mixture of salt, herbs, and spices. Use
a piece of gut or wire to tie the forelegs to
the neck. Fasten the lamb to the spit,
securing it in 3 places with steel wire.
Stretch the hind legs out along the spit. Melt
the butter and margarine in a pot with the
oil. Season with the same mixture of salt,
herbs, and spices as above. Brush the lamb
with this mixture and pour the remainder
into a shallow pan 1 m (good 3′) long, 30 cm
(1′) wide, and 5 cm (2″) deep. Place this
improvised drip pan beside the fire trench
just under the spit.

Hoist the spitted lamb onto the supports
and roast for about 3 hours. Do not try to
keep the spit turning; give it a quarter turn
every 5 minutes. Using a large spoon lashed
securely to a stick, baste the lamb every 15
minutes with the contents of the drip pan.
After 2 hours wrap the midsection in
aluminum foil— it browns much faster than
the shoulders and legs. Méchoui is perfectly
cooked when small fissures appear in the
meat and the skin on the legs becomes
crackled.

You can eat méchoui in the traditional
way, with your hands directly from the spit
(remember to set out finger bowls), or you
can carve and serve it more conventionally.
In this case, the crisp skin is usually served
with the ribs, shoulders, sides, and hind
legs. The undercut of the loin is generally
not served because it becomes overdone

and shrivelled. Served with salade niçoise
(Recipe 69) and washed down with a cool
wine, your feast should be a great success.

205. Stuffing for Méchoui

3 kg (6 1/2 lb) shell macaroni
1 kg (2 1/4 lb) black olives
2 buds garlic
1 sprig basil *or* 1 tbsp dried basil
2 sprigs mint *or* 2 tbsp dried mint
1 kg (2 1/4 lb) onions
250 g (8 oz) fresh parsley *or* 60 g (2 oz)
    dried parsley
3 tbsp cayenne
1 tbsp cumin
1 tbsp anise seed
1 tbsp iodized sea salt

Cook the macaroni for 10 minutes in very
salty water. Remove the tongue, brains,
testicles, heart, liver, and lungs from the
lamb along with the lean trimmings after
dressing it. Chop and mix all the ingredients
together, including the cooked pasta. Stuff
the lamb before fastening it to the spit.

Note: As you can see, this recipe is practical
only if you slaughter your own lamb or at
least have a good deal to do with the
process. But unstuffed méchoui is perfectly
respectable.

206. Spit-Roasted Young Goat

Serves 8

2 cloves garlic
2 green onions
Bunch fresh herbs (wild thyme, basil,
    oregano), shredded with scissors,
    ***or* 1 tbsp of these herbs, dried**
100 ml (1/3 cup) olive oil
60 ml (1/4 cup) cognac
Juice of 1 lemon
Salt, fresh-ground white pepper
1 young goat (delicious from March until
    May)

Crush the garlic, onions, and herbs in a mortar. Moisten this paste with oil, cognac, and lemon juice. Season generously with salt and pepper.

Brush the kid inside and out with this mixture, then pour the remainder into the drip pan. Secure the kid to a spit and roast over a medium fire for 45 minutes, basting every 5 minutes.

ORGAN MEAT

207. Spit-Roasted Calf's Liver

Serves 4

1 piece calf's liver, 1.2 kg (2 1/2 lb)
Salt, white pepper
1 pork caul*
Butter, melted
2 carrots, sliced in rounds
1 onion, quartered
Bouquet garni
5 stalks fresh tarragon *or* 5 tbsp dried
    tarragon
250 ml (1 cup) dry white wine
Sauce Diable (Recipe 39)

Season the liver with salt and pepper. Wrap in the caul and brush with melted butter. Place the carrots, onion, bouquet garni, tarragon, and wine in the drip pan.

Place the liver on a spit, making sure that it is tightly gripped between the prongs. Turn over a gentle fire for 20 minutes, basting every 5 minutes. Serve with Sauce Diable.

*See note to Recipe 127.

VEGETABLE, CHEESE, AND FRUIT

208. Roast Corn on the Cob

Serves 4

**8 tender ears corn, with the husks and
    silk removed
Butter, melted
Sweet *or* salted butter
Salt**

Coat the corn with melted butter. Cook
over a low heat for 15 minutes. Either
season with salt and serve with sweet butter
or serve with salted butter.

209. Raclette Shepherd Style

Serves 8

3.2 kg (7 lb) raclette cheese

Divide the cheese into 8 portions, 400 g
(scant 1 lb) each. Everyone should place
their portions of cheese on a long-handled
knife and hold them over the barbecue until
the cheese begins to melt, then scrape off
the melted part with another knife and eat it
at once.

This is the earliest way of eating raclette,
invented many centuries ago by the Swiss
shepherds of the Valais.

210. Barbecued Pineapple

Serves 6

**1 large pineapple, not too ripe
250 ml (1 cup) dark rum
6 tbsp brown sugar**

Peel the pineapple but leave it whole.
Marinate in the rum for 2 hours, giving it a
quarter turn every 10 minutes. Sprinkle
with brown sugar and put on a spit. Cook
for 10 minutes over a gentle fire, basting
with rum and sprinkling with brown sugar
so that an even caramel coating is formed.

IX

COOKING IN FOIL

FISH AND SEAFOOD

211. Salmon Steaks in Foil

Serves 4

50 g (1 3/4 oz) mushrooms
2 shallots
1 clove garlic
2 tbsp fresh dill *or* **2 tsp dried dill**
Salt, white pepper
Butter
4 thick slices fresh salmon
Dry white wine
Lemon juice

Chop the mushrooms, shallots, garlic, and dill together and season with salt and pepper.

Butter 4 squares of aluminum foil. Divide half the chopped mixture among them, then place on each a salmon steak seasoned with salt and pepper. Spread the remainder of the chopped mixture over the fish and moisten with wine and lemon juice. Seal the aluminum foil and place on the barbecue. Grill for 6 minutes on each side.

212. Fish in Foil Peking Style

Serves 4

12 fish fillets, about 50 g (1 3/4 oz) each;
select your fish according to the
season and your market
Salt, white pepper
Sherry
Lard
Fresh ginger, peeled and thinly sliced, *or*
ground ginger
Snow peas
Young green onions, cut into pieces
Mushrooms, thinly sliced

Season the fillets with salt and pepper and sprinkle with sherry. Grease 4 pieces of aluminum foil with lard and divide the fillets among them.

On each fillet of fish place a thin slice of ginger, a pea pod, a piece of green onion, and a slice of mushroom. Seal the foil carefully and place on the grill. Cook for 10 minutes without turning.

213. Red Mullet in Foil

Serves 4

**8 red mullet,* very fresh
1 bunch basil *or* 2 tsp dried basil
1 tbsp anchovy paste
2 tbsp olive oil
Pepper**

Scale the mullet but do not clean them; remove nothing but the gills. Rinse well and wipe dry. Heat the grill. Crush about 10 basil leaves to a paste in a mortar with the anchovy paste and oil. Add a few whole leaves of basil or dried basil.

   Season the mullet with pepper, coat with the basil and anchovy sauce, and place on a sheet of aluminum foil. Cover with a second sheet, seal the edges securely, and place on a very hot grill. Cook for 4 minutes on each side.

   *See note to Recipe 81.

214. Shrimp with Anise

Serves 4

200 g (7 oz) *crème fraîche
50 ml (scant 1/4 cup) anise liquor (Pernod *or* Ricard)
Ground ginger
Salt, white pepper
1 sprig fresh chervil, finely chopped, *or* 1 tbsp dried chervil
3–6 large shrimp per person, according to size**

Whisk together the cream, liquor, ginger, salt, pepper, and chervil. In each of 4 squares of aluminum foil place a serving of shrimp and a quarter of the anise-flavored cream. Seal the foil and grill on the barbecue for 4 minutes on each side. Serve very hot.

   *See note to Recipe 28.

POULTRY AND GAME

215. Breast of Chicken in Foil

Per person

Oil
50 g (1 3/4 oz) mushrooms, finely chopped
1 tsp finely chopped onion
1 tsp finely chopped shallot
Salt, white pepper
Nutmeg
1/2 tsp dry white wine
1/2 tsp lemon juice
1/2 chicken breast, 200 g (scant 1/2 lb), boned, skinned, and trimmed
2 small bards*

Oil a rectangular piece of doubled aluminum foil. Thoroughly mix the chopped vegetables; season with salt, pepper, and nutmeg and moisten with the wine and lemon juice. Divide the mixture in two.

Season the chicken breast with salt and pepper. Lay a bard on the foil, spread it with half the chopped vegetables, and place the chicken on top; cover the chicken with the second half of the vegetables and finish with the second bard. Seal the packet tightly, place on the grill, and cook for 20 minutes, turning once.

*See note 2 to Recipe 201.

216. Young Pigeon in Foil

Per person

1 young pigeon, cleaned and singed, including the liver
1 tsp each chopped fresh parsley, chives, basil, and shallot *or* pinch each of these herbs, dried
Salt, fresh-ground white pepper
1 clove garlic, finely crushed in a mortar
50 ml (1 3/4 oz) oil
1 tbsp dry white wine
Lime juice

Chop the pigeon liver and add it to the chopped herbs. Add salt, pepper, and the garlic and mix in the oil. Turn the mixture into a deep bowl and marinate the pigeon in it for 4 hours in a cool place, turning often.

Place the pigeon, coated with the marinade, in the center of a large piece of doubled aluminum foil. Raise the edges of the foil, then pour the wine around the bird; add a few drops of lime juice. Seal the foil tightly and place the packet in the coals for 10 minutes. Serve in the foil.

PORK

217. Pork Chops in Foil

Serves 4

**4 thick, boneless rib chops *or* very thick
    butterfly chops**
Fresh-ground black pepper
16 very thin slices bacon
Fresh sage leaves *or* 2 tsp dried sage
4 leaves fresh mint *or* 1 tsp dried mint

Cut 4 rectangles of aluminum foil large
enough to completely enclose a chop.
Pepper the chops on both sides. On each
piece of aluminum foil place 4 slices of
bacon, then the chops; sprinkle them with
sage. Add 1 leaf of fresh mint, or a small
pinch of dried mint, to each chop; it will
develop the scent of the sage.

Roll the chops up in the foil and seal the
ends well. Place on the coals and cook for
30 minutes, turning from time to time. Serve
in the foil as they are.

218. Sausages Normandes in Foil

Serves 4

100 ml (1/3 cup) dry cider
4 tbsp *crème fraîche**
1 tbsp prepared hot mustard
2 pinches cinnamon
2 pinches white pepper
4 pinches salt
**1 choice eating apple, cut into thin slivers
    (julienned)**
4 white sausages *or* pork sausages

Mix the cider, cream, mustard, spices, and
salt together. Add the apple. Coat 4 pieces of
aluminum foil with the cider cream and
wrap 1 sausage in each. Cook for 20 minutes
on the grill, turning from time to time.

*See note to Recipe 28.

VEAL

219. Veal Cutlets in Foil

Serves 4

Butter
4 veal cutlets, 200 g (scant 1/2 lb) each
Salt, white pepper
200 g (7 oz) mushrooms, very thinly sliced
4 tomatoes, peeled, seeded, crushed, and
   drained if necessary
100 g (3 1/2 oz) ham, very finely chopped
2 tbsp fresh basil, shredded with scissors,
   or **2 tsp dried basil**

Lightly butter 4 pieces of aluminum foil, which should be large enough to completely enclose a cutlet. Season the meat with salt and pepper and place on the foil. On each cutlet spread a quarter of the mushrooms, tomatoes, ham, and basil.

Seal the foil and place the packets on a very hot barbecue. Grill for 8 minutes on each side. Serve them opened on individual plates.

220. Veal Chops in Foil with Morels

Serves 4

**4 veal rib chops, each 250 g (1/2 lb),
   deboned
Salt, white pepper
Butter, melted
200 g (7 oz) fresh morels* *or* 1 small packet
   dried morels, soaked for 3 hours in
   warm water
8 bards**
16 leaves fresh sage *or* 1 1/2 tbsp dried
   sage
8 leaves fresh mint *or* 2 tsp dried mint
Dry white wine**

Season the veal with salt and pepper and
brush with melted butter. Blanch the morels
in boiling, salted water.

Lay 1 bard on a rectangle of aluminum
foil; on this place 2 sage leaves and 1 mint
leaf, then the veal chop, another 2 sage
leaves and 1 mint leaf, and a second bard.
Sprinkle with wine and a quarter of the
morels. Seal the foil. Repeat for the 3 other
cutlets. Place on the grill and cook for 30
minutes, turning often.

*One of the world's great natural delicacies,
   these unique mushrooms cannot be
   cultivated, so the supply is expensive and
   unpredictable. Luckily, they are not
   confined to Europe, so if you learn to
   recognize them you may find them in May
   or June at the spot where woods and
   meadows meet.
**See note 2 to Recipe 201.

LAMB

221. Lamb Chops with Seven Herbs

Serves 4

Fresh *or* dried rosemary, thyme, savory, bay, sage, mint, and basil
Olive oil
Salt, fresh-ground pepper
8 lamb rib chops

Use dried herbs or crush the fresh herbs to a paste in a mortar; use equal amounts of rosemary, thyme, and savory and smaller quantities of the rest. You need 4 tbsp of paste. Bind the paste with oil and season generously with salt and pepper.

Coat the chops completely with this aromatic mixture and seal them tightly in aluminum foil. Place on very hot coals and grill for 5 minutes on each side.

222. Leg of Lamb in Foil

Butter
4 anchovy fillets
4 slices cooked ham
2 onions
4 sour pickled gherkins
Parsley, chopped
Thyme flowers *or* dried thyme
Fresh *or* dried mint *or* oregano
Salt, white pepper
1 leg of lamb, larded* with pork fat and raw ham
200 ml (scant 1 cup) dry white wine
Juice of 1 lemon

Butter a large sheet of tripled aluminum foil. Chop together the anchovy fillets, ham, onions, gherkins, parsley, thyme, mint, salt, and pepper.

Rub the lamb with salt and pepper. Butter it well and sear it over the barbecue for 10 minutes on each side. Place it on the aluminum foil and spread it with the savory mixture. Raise the edges of the foil and pour the wine and lemon juice around the meat. Seal the foil tightly. Place it on the barbecue and grill for 2 hours.

*See note to Recipe 195.

ORGAN MEAT

223. Tripe in Foil

Serves 4

**600 g (generous 1 1/4 lb) blanched best
   tripe, coarsely ground
250 ml (1 cup) breadcrumbs
2 tomatoes, peeled, seeded, and crushed
1 clove garlic, crushed
1 egg yolk
4 tbsp prepared hot mustard
1 tbsp lard plus a litle lard to grease the foil
Juice of 1 lemon
Salt, white pepper
Nutmeg
Cayenne**

Knead all the ingredients together thoroughly. Divide the mixture into 8 equal parts and form into flat patties. Lightly grease 8 squares of aluminum foil with lard and seal 1 patty in each piece. Place on the grill and cook for 10 minutes on each side. Serve with either pepper sauce (Recipe 20) or anchoïade (Recipe 51).

VEGETABLES

224. Mushrooms in Foil

Serves 4

12 *cèpes** (boletus mushrooms) *or* 12 very
   large cultivated mushrooms
Parsley, chopped
Salt, white pepper

Use only the mushroom caps. Clean them
thoroughly without washing them. Cut 12
squares of aluminum foil and place 1
mushroom cap upside down on each. Dust
with a mixture of parsley, salt, and pepper.
Seal the foil tightly and place the packets on
the coals for a scant 30 minutes. Serve
immediately.

   *See note to Recipe 136.

225. Potatoes with Roquefort in Foil

Serves 4

1 kg (2 1/4 lb) potatoes
Salt, fresh-ground white pepper
Paprika
Oil
200 g (7 oz) Roquefort cheese
100 g (3 1/2 oz) butter
100 g (3 1/2 oz) raw ham, chopped

Wash and peel the potatoes and wipe them
dry. Cut into thick rounds. Season with salt,
pepper, and paprika. Divide among 4 oiled
pieces of aluminum foil.

   Beat together the cheese, butter, and ham.
Season with pepper. Spread this mixture
over the potato rounds and seal the packets
well. Cook for 40 minutes on the grill,
turning frequently.

226. Potatoes with Herbs

Serves 4

8 well-shaped, uniform potatoes
1 stalk fresh chervil *or* 1 tbsp dried chervil
1 stalk fresh tarragon *or* 1 tbsp dried
** tarragon**
1 stalk fresh chives *or* 1 tbsp dried chives
1 stalk fresh mint *or* 1 tbsp dried mint
1 stalk fresh parsley *or* 1 tbsp dried parsley
200 g (7 oz) *crème fraîche**
Salt, cayenne pepper

Wash and peel the potatoes and wipe them
dry. Cut them in two lengthwise and scoop
out a hollow in each half. Chop the herbs
together and beat them into the cream.
Season with salt and cayenne pepper.

  Fill the hollows of the potatoes with this
cream. Put each potato back together and
wrap tightly in aluminum foil. Cook in the
coals for 40 minutes.

  *See note to Recipe 28.

CHEESE AND FRUIT

227. Chabichous in Foil

Serves 4

**4 chabichous (small goat's milk cheese
from the Poitou region of France),
rather dry
4 tbsp olive oil
2 pinches cayenne
20 black peppercorns, crushed
1 tbsp fresh rosemary *or* 1 tsp dried
rosemary
1 tsp fresh savory *or* pinch dried savory
1 tsp fresh tarragon, shredded with
scissors, *or* pinch dried tarragon
1 tsp fresh thyme flowers *or* pinch dried
thyme**

Leave the chabichous to soak for 2 hours
with all the other ingredients.

Cut 4 squares of aluminum foil. In the
center of each place 1 chabichou, still
drenched with the marinade. Seal the foil.
Place on the barbecue and grill for 5
minutes on each side. Serve with toasted
whole wheat bread and with a mill of black
pepper on the table.

228. Pineapple in Foil

Serves 6

**1 fresh pineapple
Light rum
4 bananas
Lime juice
Vanilla sugar
Butter
Brown sugar**

Peel the pineapple and cut it into slices, not
too thick. Soak for 2 hours in light rum. Peel
the bananas and crush them with a fork,
sprinkling them with lime juice and vanilla
sugar. Spread each slice of pineapple with
banana and top with a second slice of
pineapple.

Place on buttered aluminum foil, sprinkle
with the rum from the marinade, and seal
the foil. Place on the barbecue and grill for
10 minutes on each side. Serve in the foil,
sprinkled with brown sugar.

229. Oranges in Foil with Alcohol

Per person

1 orange
1 tsp sugar
1 tsp each 3 kinds of alcohol — for
 example, kirsch, maraschino, gin

Peel an orange completely with a knife. Cut crosswise into slices about 1.5 cm (1/2″) thick and sprinkle each slice with sugar, then put the orange back together.

Place on a double sheet of aluminum foil; raise the edges and sprinkle the orange with a mixture of the chosen alcohol, then seal the foil tightly. Bury the packet in the coals for 15 minutes. Serve in the foil.

230. Apples in Foil

Per person

1 choice eating apple
Lemon juice
Pinch cinnamon
Brown sugar
Butter, melted

Peel and core the apple, sprinkling it immediately with lemon juice. Place on a piece of doubled aluminum foil. Dust with cinnamon and fill the core with brown sugar. Brush with melted butter and seal the foil tightly. Bury the packet in the coals for 20 minutes.

Index Of Recipes
By Main Ingredient

Note: The numbers given are recipe numbers, not page numbers.

Beef

Beef Tenderloin with Herbes de Provence, 110

Brochette Medley, 180

Brochettes of Beef with Artichokes, 165

Butcher's Tenderloin with Shallots, 119

Chilean Entrecôtes, 113

Contre-Filet Périgord Style, 112

Entrecôtes Tuscan Style, 114

Grilled Beef Rolls, 122

Grilled Sirloin Tip with Chipolatas, 117

Grilled Sirloin with Roquefort Butter, 118

Hamburgers with Mint, 121

Hungarian Mixed Grill, 132

Jouquard Brochettes, 166

Mexican Rolls, 168

Mixed Grill Supreme, 133

Peking Grill, 120

Portuguese Brochettes, 167

Rib of Beef Niçoise, 116

Rib of Beef with Anchoïade, 115

Spit-Roasted Beef Tenderloin, 200

Spit-Roasted Beef Tongue, 201

Spit-Roasted Contre-Filet, 202

Tournedos on Slate, 111

Cheese

Barbecued Cheeses, 140

Chabichous in Foil, 227

Cheddar Brochettes in Five Flavors, 185

Cheese Mixed Grill, 141

Raclette, 142

Raclette Shepherd Style, 209

Fish

Barbecued Herring, 79

Barbecued Sole, 84

Barbecued Trout, 74

Ceviche Polynesian Style, 50

Conger Eel Spanish Style, 146

Fish in Foil Peking Style, 212

Fruit

Game and Venison

Lamb